Forestry in Development Planning

Forestry in Development Planning

Lessons from the Rural Experience

Harry W. Blair
and Porus D. Olpadwala

LONDON AND NEW YORK

First published 1988 by Westview Press

Published 2018 by Routledge
52 Vanderbilt Avenue, New York, NY 10017
2 Park Square, Milton Park, Abingdon, Oxon OX14 4RN

Routledge is an imprint of the Taylor & Francis Group, an informa business

Copyright © 1988 by Taylor & Francis

All rights reserved. No part of this book may be reprinted or reproduced or utilised in any form or by any electronic, mechanical, or other means, now known or hereafter invented, including photocopying and recording, or in any information storage or retrieval system, without permission in writing from the publishers.

Notice:
Product or corporate names may be trademarks or registered trademarks, and are used only for identification and explanation without intent to infringe.

Library of Congress Catalog Card Number: 88-14259

ISBN 13: 978-0-367-01415-5 (hbk)
ISBN 13: 978-0-367-16402-7 (pbk)

CONTENTS

LIST OF FIGURES   x
PREFACE   xi

PART I. INTRODUCTION   1

CHAPTER 1. OVERVIEW   3
    A. Rural Development and Forestry   3
    B. Social Forestry in Gujarat, India   6
    C. An Overview and Some Definitions   11

PART II. CONSTRAINTS TO DEVELOPMENT: LIMITS TO CHANGE   13

CHAPTER 2. RESOURCE CONSTRAINTS   15
    A. Natural, Human and Financial Resources   15
    B. The Unique Case of Time as a Special Natural Resource   18

CHAPTER 3. ORGANIZATIONAL CONSTRAINTS   21
    A. Within the Organization   21
    B. Linkages Between Organization and Environment   31
    C. Ignoring Indigenous Rural Knowledge and Priorities   32

CHAPTER 4. POLICY CONSTRAINTS   37
    A. Policies Favoring Urban Over Rural Interests   38
    B. Policies Concentrating Rather than Redistributing Income   42
    C. Policies Displacing Labor   45
    D. Policies Favoring the "External" Over the "Internal"   48
    E. Equity and Efficiency in Development Policy   48

CHAPTER 5. STRUCTURAL AND SYSTEM CONSTRAINTS   55
    A. Structural Constraints at the Local Level   55
    B. Structural Constraints at the National Level   57
    C. Linkages Between National and Local Levels   58
    D. System Constraints   60

PART III. TACKLING THE CONSTRAINTS: DEVELOPMENT INITIATIVES 67

CHAPTER 6. RURAL INSTITUTIONS AND DEVELOPMENT 69
A. The Universe of Rural Institutions and the Central Importance of Local Organizations 69

B. Types of Local Organizations 74

C. The Role of Participation 82

D. Rural Institutions, Local Organizations, Participation and Forestry 85

CHAPTER 7. RURAL DEVELOPMENT STRATEGIES 89
A. The Spectrum of Institutional Change 89

B. Adaptive Development Administration 92

C. Public Choice, Privatization and Collective Action 97

D. Decentralization 103

E. Farming Systems Research and the Training and Visit System 107

CHAPTER 8. EQUITY AND BALANCE IN RURAL INSTITUTIONS 115
A. Employment Creation and Technological Change 115

B. Regional and Area Development 124

C. Women in Rural Development 128

D. Forestry and Rural Equity 131

CHAPTER 9. LESSONS IN RURAL DEVELOPMENT: SOME ILLUSTRATIONS 137
A. The Comilla Project in Bangladesh 137

B. Community Development and Panchayati Raj in India 141

C. The Anand Milk Producers' Union (Amul) in India 145

D. Ujamaa in Tanzania (by Louise Fortmann) 150

E. A Producers' Cooperative in Rural Bolivia (by Kevin Healy) 152

PART IV. FITTING FORESTRY AND RURAL DEVELOPMENT TOGETHER 157

CHAPTER 10. POTENTIAL PITFALLS FOR FORESTRY IN DEVELOPMENT 159
    A. "Building on the Best" as an Extension Strategy   159
    B. Cash-cropping Biomass at the Expense of Food Crops   161
    C. Shrinking Rather than Providing Employment   163
    D. People, Governments and the Legacy of History   165

CHAPTER 11. CONCLUSION 169

ABBREVIATIONS AND ACRONYMS 173

REFERENCES 175

INDEX OF NAMES 199

INDEX OF SUBJECTS 203

FIGURES

1. Rural Institutions Located Along Three Dimensions   71

2. Types of Local Organizations (LOs)   76

3. Task Areas of Rural Institutions   78

4. The Spectrum of Institutional Change   91

5. Goods and Services Classified by Consumption and Excludability   100

6. The Cycle of Economic Growth and Its Break Points   117

PREFACE

This project started in a sense at the beginning of the 1980s with two disparate experiences of the authors. Harry Blair had a leave of absence from his university post to work at the United States Agency for International Development, where he became involved in several project plans for natural resource management. Porus Olpadwala served twice as a guest lecturer at the World Conference on Agrarian Reform and Rural Development project at the headquarters of the Food and Agricultural Organization of the United Nations in Rome, and in the course of these visits exchanged ideas with several people in the FAO Forestry Department. As a result of these experiences, both of us became quite interested in forestry, particularly in its then-new manifestation of social forestry and how some of the thinking we had absorbed (and argued with) at Cornell University's Center for International Studies might relate to this new field of development endeavor.

Then in 1982 the authors were asked by the FAO's Forestry Department to do a brief analysis focusing on lessons that the overall experience in rural development might have for social forestry. Our paper led to a month at the FAO in Rome during the summer of 1982 and a longer paper finished midway through 1984. Since then we have expanded our ideas considerably, dropped some and added others, to the extent that the present offering has only a vague resemblance to what we started with six years ago.

Along the way we have accumulated many debts to a wide number of people who have encouraged and supported us. Institutionally, our greatest debt is to the Rural Development Committee at Cornell University, which supported the early part of our enterprise both financially and intellectually. In addition, Harry Blair received support in various ways from the American Institute of Indian Studies and the Social Science Research Council, the School of Forestry and Environmental Science at Yale University and the Department of Rural Sociology at Cornell, and the Scholarly Development Comittee at Bucknell University. Porus Olpadwala received support from the City and Regional Planning Department at Cornell.

The list of individuals that advised, assisted, argued with and guided us is long and we could never name all the people who helped us in crucial ways. We do wish, however, to record first of all our thanks to Milton Esman and Norman Uphoff of Cornell for their steady influence and encouragement throughout our effort. Peter May of Cornell's Rural Development Committee helped us with several early drafts, and a small section of his handiwork survives as a section of Chapter 6. We are most grateful to Louise Fortmann of the Forestry Department at the University of California, Berkeley, and to Kevin Healy of the Inter-American Foundation for letting us reprint two of their essays that appeared in Cornell's *Rural Development Participation Review*. Gerry Finen and Jim Riker, both of Cornell's Government Department, gave us much help with research and references.

And finally we wish also to thank, for their help, guidance and willingness to argue with us: Mike Arnold, Oxford Forestry Institute; Zarina Bhatty, USAID India; Bill Burch, Yale Forestry School; C. Chandrasekharan, FAO Forestry Department; Eric Chetwynd, Office of Rural Development, USAID; Mafa Chipeta, FAO Forestry Department; Ed Connerly, National Association of Schools of Public Affairs and Administration; Diana Conyers, University College of Swansea, U.K.; Hal Fisher, USAID India; Ramachandra Guha, Indian Scientific Institute, Bangalore; Chuck Hatch, Forestry School, University of Idaho; Ken Kornher, Office of Rural Development, USAID; David Korten, USAID Indonesia; Tom Mehen, Office of Rural Development, USAID; Al Merkel, USAID Pakistan; Arvind Reddy, Maharashtra Forestry Department; Jeff Romm, Berkeley Forestry School; Mike Savonis, City and Regional Planning, Cornell; and Suzanne Wallen, Rural Sociology, Cornell.

Harry W. Blair
Lewisburg, PA

Porus D. Olpadwala
Ithaca, NY

Forestry in
Development Planning

PART I

INTRODUCTION

After long isolation from its sister disciplines in the sphere of rural development, forestry has in the last decade emerged from its concentration on conservation and production practiced largely in remote areas to a wider focus embracing an outreach to the general rural population. Inasmuch as the other sectors involved in the rural development effort over the past three or four decades had a considerable head start, it follows that they have built up a good reservoir of experience both good and bad, which forestry in its new expansion of interest could tap.

In this introductory chapter, we explore some of that relationship between forestry and rural development, then briefly examine a single social forestry project to see how it would look from a rural development perspective. Finally, we endeavor to nail down a few definitions for terms we will be employing as we go on.

CHAPTER 1. OVERVIEW

A. Rural Development and Forestry

In the period since the Second World War and the gaining of independence by the African and Asian countries, there has been much money, planning, intellectual effort and administrative energy directed toward promoting social and economic development in the area now known as the Third World -- the less developed countries or LDCs of Africa, the Americas, Asia and, more recently, the relatively newly independent states of Oceania. During the earlier years of this effort to bring about development, the focus was mainly on the industrial and urban sectors, with the countryside seen largely as a resource base that would provide much of the manpower, the funding and some of the foreign exchange needed to direct the national development effort. In the typical texts dealing with the new field of economic development during the 1950s and 1960s, a chapter or two at most might be given to the agricultural sector and virtually no space to all the other human activity taking place in the rural areas where as many as 90 percent of an LDC's population might be living.

In the middle 1960s and subsequent years, however, two things happened to change these guiding ideas. First, there was increasing concern with the prospect of widespread famine, mostly centering at that time on the North Indian famine of 1965-67, which put well over a hundred million people at risk. Second, it was just about at this time that the long work involved in creating "Green Revolution" technologies for increasing foodgrain yields became ready for use. These two factors combined to prompt a change of focus on the part of developers to include a much larger agricultural emphasis.

By the early 1970s the agricultural emphasis had begun to pay off with substantially increased foodgrain production in many LDCs. But at the same time it was becoming clear that the benefits of agricultural growth had not "trickled down" very far into rural society. Indeed, the majority of the rural population in most Third World countries fell far below any reasonable minimum income or nutritional standards. The results of economic growth, in other words, were going largely to those who had most of the rural wealth and power already. It was in this atmosphere that the various programs of "redistribution with growth," "new directions," "basic human needs" and the like were launched -- to bring development to the "poor rural majority" that had thus far been left out of whatever economic growth had taken place.

This enlargement of the development mission in the countryside meant that a number of other sectors beside agriculture had to be brought into play. The poor rural majority could not be attended to without involvement of health and education departments, for example, and even within agriculture the focus moved beyond agronomy to encompass such areas as animal husbandry, extension, agricultural credit and water management.

Today, development efforts in the international donor community have become overlaid with projects to promote such strategies as privatization, decentralization and farming systems research, but a central emphasis remains on the poor rural majority. And in the process of this sequence of concerns over three decades and more, initiatives and policy changes, a corpus of theory and practice grew up that is now usually referred to as "rural development," or RD. This corpus contains a long history of failed projects and abstract analyses of what went wrong, but it also includes a growing body of knowledge of what has worked and why.

Until quite recently forestry both as a practice and as an intellectual discipline has not been part of rural development, mostly for historical reasons. As modern forestry took shape in the late 19th and early 20th centuries, its major missions of resource conservation and sustained yield production were geographically centered in regions away from those where agriculture was practiced. Indeed, the goal of conservation was best attained in part by keeping agriculture and agriculturalists at a distance, both physically and intellectually. Thus even today, in most of the American states, the state forestry school is quite distinct from the state agriculture school, often to the extent that the two are on different campuses altogether. And where forestry has become a part of the development enterprise, it tends to retain a separate identity, as for instance in the FAO itself, where the Forestry Department is situated in a building at a considerable distance from the main headquarters housing the agriculture-related departments (and a commuter bus is used to connect the two).

Two central concerns of the 1970s brought forestry as a field into the international development picture. The first was the environmental concentration on deforestation and allied problems of soil erosion and flood control that gained widespread attention in that decade. In some areas the basic forest resource itself seemed in danger of disappearing altogether and in many others it was clearly under severe pressure as increasing populations ravaged ever greater numbers of trees for fuel and fodder supplies. The second factor was the successive oil shocks that inspired concerted efforts to find alternative sources of energy. One of the most obvious options was fuelwood, which did not need the lengthy research and development effort that solar power schemes like photovoltaic cells were going to take, nor did it take on the controversy surrounding nuclear power as an alternative to fossil fuels.

The result of this interest has been an explosion in forestry projects for development in the LDCs. As of the early 1980s, by one estimate (Foley and Barnard, 1984: 217-223) there were over 130 forestry development projects in place in Third World countries, slated to spend more than $US 750 million in external grants and loans from eleven international donors in the course of completion.[1] And the total task will unquestionably be much larger; the World Resources Institute, for example, recently (WRI, 1985: I, 24ff) called for some $US 1.9 billion to be committed to forestry development efforts in 32 crucial countries over a five-year period.

As the forestry sector has taken up activities in such areas as agroforestry, community forestry and reforestation, is has not surprisingly run into many of the same situations as RD has experienced over the last thirty years. Projects are abandoned by their supposed beneficiaries, implementing bureaucracies are unresponsive to the new challenges posed by social forestry, research cells are totally out of touch with the practical problems they are supposed to be working on, extension agents seem unable to communicate with villagers, and projects when they do meet targets somehow seem to benefit the local rich rather than the poor rural majority.

In fact, all these problems and many more have been faced by RD projects, sometimes successfully and oftentimes quite otherwise. The outcome of this long track record of success and failure is a rich experience of theory and practice that can and should be most valuable to those in the forestry sector. This is so for the obvious reason that the one can learn from the other's triumphs and disasters, but it is also true for the more subtle reason that forestry is now in a situation where it cannot function successfully without becoming a part of the overall RD environment. When forestry was practiced more or less exclusively on isolated tracts of reserved lands, it could afford to ignore its human environment, though not without considerable cost, as alienated forest dwellers contributed their own depredations to the overall deforestation process. But when forestry took on the tasks of social forestry programs, it had to deal with the rural population outside the reserved forest areas. This much larger population had to be convinced of the worth of the ideas that foresters were now presenting; it could not be ordered about as had forest dwellers (however ineffectual such management practices may have been).

In short, forestry can no longer be practiced in isolation from the general RD enterprise. As Romm (1986) points out, forest policy cannot be pursued apart from the socio-economic environment in which it must function. Instead, that policy must be charted in relation to and as a part of that environment. Villagers grow (or abandon or destroy) trees on the same logic that they employ to grow foodcrops, sharecrop land, sink a tubewell or gather cropwastes for cooking fuel. They do not distinguish between a forestry sector to deal with trees and a RD sector to handle everything else. Thus if forestry is to become a functioning part of the total development effort in the LDCs, it must integrate itself into that effort.

To give a more concrete idea of the linkages between rural development and forestry, and to begin to look at the forestry sector from a rural development perspective, it would make sense to look briefly at an example. The Social Forestry Project in India's Gujarat state offers an excellent case study in this regard, for it is one of the more outstanding stories in the whole field of development forestry. It illustrates a number of the more successful approaches in RD, and at the same time its less impressive aspects also point to similar RD experiences.

B. Social Forestry in Gujarat, India

Whenever the topic of social forestry comes up, the work of the Community Forestry Wing (CFW) of the Gujarat state government's Forest Department is invariably mentioned as one of the real success stories of the field. To start with, the project has planted a larger number of trees with greater speed and enthusiasm than has any similar project so far. But more significantly in our context, the Gujarat experience has a number of lessons to offer, both positive and negative, from the rural development perspective. There are several aspects of the CFW's success that fit in very well with what has worked over the years in RD, while at the same time there are some definite problems with the Gujarat effort that also mirror what has often gone awry in RD enterprises. Both lessons and cautionary tales will be taken up in this brief account.[2]

An outline of the story is easily told. Beginning in 1969 as a state-sponsored endeavor, the project built up its experience for a decade until 1979, when the World Bank entered the picture as an outside sponsor. Since then the project has made tremendous strides. It quickly exceeded its already ambitious targets for strip plantations and village woodlots, and met them in reforesting degraded forestland. Although this is a creditable accomplishment by itself, the project gets its real acclaim from its farm forestry component. Here it more than doubled the target by the second year, and by 1983 was distributing almost four times the target number of seedlings, planting almost 200 million on private holdings throughout the state. In fact, the project has become so successful that just possibly the state's growing needs for forestry products might be met within a decade.

The program has reached out to small farmers as well as big ones. In the first year there were almost 16,500 participants in farm forestry who owned less than 2 hectares, and by the third year the number more than tripled to over 53,000. Further, the project has generated a considerable amount of employment: more than 16 million workdays during its first two-and-a-half years, with over a third of the total going to women. These are outstanding achievements indeed.

Community forestry also deserves particular mention. At the end of the program's third year, some 3,500 village woodlot projects had been initiated, each one on the common land of a village panchayat (the local self-governing body at village level in India). Averaging about five hectares in size, the projects generally involve four-year cycles, with poles, fuelwood and some fodder being the main objectives. The CFW furnishes the management and inputs for most of these projects, with the panchayat supplying the plant protection. At harvesting, the CFW deducts costs and gives half the produce to the panchayat.

There are at least two aspects of the CFW experience that tally with what has been learned over the years in RD. The first is that *success took a considerable time to come about*. True, the World Bank-sponsored project very quickly became an exemplar of community forestry, but the real effort by the CFW began a full decade earlier. This ten year period had many frustrations and setbacks, as the CFW slowly learned the arts of extension, promotion, training and in general how to relate to people outside the traditional domain of the forester.[3] Then in 1979 the project was ready to take off, and did. But without the long experimentation phase, success would undoubtedly have been much more difficult to attain.

The second lesson stems from the first and centers on the CFW's *ability to use the project as a learning experience* over the years. Foresters working on the project saw it an opportunity in it to learn from failure in the initial years, and as a result continuously redesigned and refocused the enterprise until they finally developed a highly successful approach. Part of this adaptability came from a willingness, at least to some extent, to learn from farmers. As soon as they received their first seedlings in the program, farmers began to experiment with different spacings, rotations, and inputs so as to develop the most profitable operation. Consequently, with their concern for recovering costs and making a profit in the short term, they hit upon a number of ideas and approaches quite different from those built up over time by the forestry establishment, with its interest in longer-term production cycles. The CFW was quick to realize this possibility for learning from farmers and in fact has put together much of its own approach for fuelwood and fodder plantations on the basis of what farmers like the legendary Kalidas Patel have pioneered.

There are also several cautionary tales that emerge from the Gujarat experience. The first is a *big farmer bias* to the program. It is true that smaller farmers have participated, and moreso here than in most social forestry programs, it is probably safe to say. Even so, there are some disturbing trends, as revealed in an FAO study done in 1983 (FAO, 1985b). It emerged in the study that while the farmers with more than 5 hectares made up 27 percent of the households surveyed, they constituted 35 percent of the households participating in the farm forestry aspect of the project and took 44 percent of the seedlings distributed. The smallest farms (those with less than one hectare), on the other hand, made up 18 percent of the households and formed 12 percent of the participants (this is a substantial achievement), but got only 7 percent of the seedlings.[4] Another survey taken at about the same time (Java, 1985; see also Agarwal and Narain, 1985: 53-54) reported similar results.

A second problem lies in *the way administrators tend to manage programs*, pressing its field agents to meet quantitative targets, if necessary at the expense of such program equity goals. Take for instance the big farmer bias in seedling distribution just mentioned above. The CFW is conscious of this problem and accordingly has made efforts to emphasize to its staff the need to bring more small farmers into the program. It has also imposed (as of the third year) a limit of 10,000 seedlings per recipient as a way of keeping large landholders from getting too big a share. Such efforts, however, can only be futile for the most part against bureaucratic pressure on CFW agents to distribute more seedlings and to assist the recipients in making sure the seedlings will survive (Mahiti Team, 1983: esp. 19-21). Clearly these targets are best achieved by giving large numbers of seedlings to a few farmers, who subsequently would be relatively easily aided to attain a high survival rate. Furthermore, since the larger and/or richer farmers are much more likely to be literate, less suspicious of outsiders and more willing (and able) to offer small and large, legal and extra-legal compensations, they are far more pleasant to deal with. From the extension forester's point of view, giving a few seedlings each to great numbers of marginal farmers is not the best way to meet targets, get good personnel evaluation reports, and/or to further one's career.

This story is an old one in the RD field, and so it is no surprise that it should be repeated here. Extension agents in every field are faced with the reality that they will be able to show much better results by dealing with a few big farmers than with many small ones. It is better for the bureaucracy (targets are met), better for the extension officer (life is easier, even more rewarding materially), and certainly better for the richer farmer strata in the countryside.

The reply of the CFW to this criticism would doubtless be that it is true to some extent, but that one has to start somewhere, and perhaps it is just as well if big farmers lead the way. They are better able to handle the risks associated with innovation, and once they have shown it can be done, the smaller and marginal farmers will join in too. Again, the same argument has been used in the RD field to justify big farmer bias, and there is more than a grain of truth to it. The problem is that by the time the smaller landholders are able to avail themselves of the new technologies, the bigger ones have taken most of the early (and large) profits, and used these gains to solidify their already dominant position. The smaller and marginal farmers are then hard pressed merely to stay in place as prices for the new commodities no longer carry a premium by the time they get their own produce to market. In Gujarat, by the time the rural poor come to take advantage of opportunities in farm forestry, the market may well be saturated.[5]

A third cause for concern in the program centers on *the types of land being used for forestry*. One of the hopes is to encourage farm forestry on marginal land, of which there is a great deal in Gujarat. Because of that, there is substantial poverty even among sizable landholders in the state. A World Bank study (Visaria, 1981) found that a large number of the 35 percent of rural households that fell below the rural "poverty line" in terms of income, had a good deal of land. Some 30 percent of the households with 3 to 4 hectares of land, for example, fell below the poverty line. That land is presumably of low quality, and not useful for agricultural crops, but there could, however, be significant possibilities for practicing farm forestry.

As things have turned out, the most successful farm forestry has normally taken place on the best land, often irrigated, where an enterprising farmer can grow a profitable eucalyptus crop in four years. This pattern fits in well with our earlier point that the nature of the extension process itself tends to bias things towards the rich farmers with better land. It also reinforces the observation that people respond to opportunity as best they can, and, in an unequal context, those with the most resources are the ones who can and do respond most adroitly, serving to worsen the income-distribution, never mind the intentions of planners and higher level RD officials. Thus good land under food crops is diverted to growing trees, while marginal and degraded land that could be put under tree species is left ignored.

The fourth word of caution deals with *employment generation.* It is noteworthy, as already observed, that in its first two and a half years the project generated some 16 million work-days of employment, of which more than one-third went to women. But what was the opportunity cost of that employment? A major motivation, in fact, for many of the farmers moving into forestry activities, was to cut down on their labor bill with a crop that only needs harvesting every four or five years. And on irrigated land, which must have been doublecropped, the saving would be even greater: one harvesting after four years as opposed to one every six months. How many million future work-days have been given up as a consequence of this current increase in employment? Clearly, from the figures mentioned, there is little justification for complacency. Although it is by no means certain that the project is eliminating more employment than it is creating, the subject definitely needs close study and monitoring.

A fifth and last concern is the *motivations people have for growing trees.* The evidence so far indicates that among both community forestry groups and individual farm foresters, there is much interest in growing poles and small timbers for commercial sale, as well as pulpwood for paper mills and fodder for animals, but virtually no enthusiasm for producing fuelwood for domestic use. What this pattern appears to reflect is the fact that while women who gather most of the cooking fuel would be the beneficiaries of an increased fuelwood supply, it is the men who make the decisions on what to market or keep for domestic use. Thus women's interests are systematically ignored and a major project goal is left unfulfilled.

Gujarat community forestry, in sum, like any RD development project, is a mixed bag. It has some real lessons for success, that could and should be emulated. But there are also some real causes for concern. Both aspects fit very much into the RD experience as it has unfolded over the last several decades.

C. An Overview and Some Definitions

The main argument of the book begins in Part II with an analysis of the context of RD, laying particular stress on the various types of constraints to development which have been identified by students of the subject so far. As we have remarked above, failures have been plentiful in RD, and there is much to be learned from them as to how and why good ideas have misfired. Once this groundwork has been laid, we then go on in Part III to analyze some of the RD strategies that have proven successful in surmounting these constraints. Later in Part III we endeavor to put some flesh on our theoretical skeleton by offering several case studies as illustrations of success and failure in implementing RD strategies. Finally in Part IV we lay out what we think are some of the major pitfalls that development forestry can avoid by taking advantage of the lessons to be derived from the RD experience. We then draw some overall conclusions.

Before getting further under way with our presentation, it would be wise to set forth a few definitions. By *development forestry* (or sometimes just "forestry") we refer to the whole spectrum of forestry as practiced in the LDCs. That is, we include both the more traditional *production forestry*, concerned primarily with its goals of sustained yield and resource conservation, and the newer field of *social forestry*, which has received so much attention and funding in recent years. Our emphasis, however, will be on the latter, for it is here that the linkages to RD are most salient.

Social forestry[6] itself we divide into two components. *Community forestry* is the growing of trees by a local organization (which may or may not be governmental in origin), on some kind of common land (village commons, government reserve land given over for the purpose, etc.), along more or less egalitarian lines. *Farm forestry*, on the other hand, consists of landowners cultivating trees on their own land, whether the land be a field that would otherwise grow foodcrops or a household compound. Other terms will be explained as we proceed.

[1] Many if not most of these projects involved host country matching commitments as well, typically on the order of 40 to 50 percent of total budget, so that in fact something over $US one billion was being spent on the forestry sector.

[2] There are by now a number of accounts of the Gujarat project, including some in the popular press (e.g., Claiborne, 1984). There are at least two by insiders (Karamchandani, 1982; Java, 1985) and one from an international source (FAO, 1985b; see also Skutsch, 1985). For an earlier analysis, see Eckholm (1979) and for a more critical assessment, see Mahiti Team (1983; also Agarwal and Narain, 1985: 53-54). The present analysis draws on all these sources, plus a field visit by Blair in 1982.

[3] Eckholm's widely cited account, for instance, was published in 1979, before the World Bank phase began.

[4] These figures given here were calculated according to what the farmers themselves reported as to their landholding size (FAO, 1985b: 29 and 75-76). When results were calculated according to the official landholding records of those included in the sample, the seedling distribution was more equal (pages 29, 32 and 37). What was occurring here was a common pattern of households owning more land in fact than was credited to them in the official record books.

[5] The FAO report speculates this may well turn out to be the case for small farmers growing poles in the hopes of getting the same premium prices that earlier farm foresters received when these products were scarce on the market (FAO, 1985b: 70; see also Claiborne, 1984).

[6] The term social forestry is a much abused one, as Foley and Barnard (1984: foreward) point out, but it has come into such widespread use that it is probably here to stay, as is evidenced by the substantial professional interest and literature that has built up. In fact there is already a well-established international network in social forestry headquartered at the Overseas Development Institute in London. Those interested in becoming a part of it should contact Dr. Gill Shepherd, Agricultural Administration Unit, Regent's College, Inner Circle, Regent's Park, London NW1 4NS, U.K. For an example of the network's activities, see Khan (1986).

PART II

CONSTRAINTS TO DEVELOPMENT: LIMITS TO CHANGE

Perhaps the most obvious and least exceptionable statement that can be made about rural development is that at any given time the process is limited or thwarted by a large number of constraints. Some of these are fully binding in that they would exist irrespective of human effort. The general climate of a region, its basic soils, and terrain are some obvious examples of these comparatively fixed constraints. There is very little that policy can do to change them, though some of their effects may be alleviated or circumvented, as through irrigation programs or land-reclamation schemes. Most constraints, however, are in one way or another person-made and therefore relatively flexible. They are, in a very real sense, institutions, for they are "patterns of activity that persist over time", although of course they are retrogressive institutions in that they impede development rather than foster it.

Constraints are dynamic and so always in a state of flux. Some become less severe over time; for instance, agricultural extension work becomes easier as a country decides to invest seriously in literacy campaigns. Others may increase or arise; if industrialized countries raise tariffs on processed raw materials in order to preserve jobs for their own workers, for example, then export market constraints for LDCs producing those materials are increased. Binding constraints are also varying. Lack of petroleum resources is not a constraint until an economy begins to use oil and gas for energy; once it does, however, the need for petroleum products in the face of shortages or price increases becomes an ever greater problem as more energy is needed. The point here is that constraints are always in a condition of change. This is true for any particular one of them, and even more true for the collectivity, with the result that the web of constraints facing the policymaker is forever shifting.

This constant flux does not mean, however, that the assessment and analysis of constraints is a waste of time. Quite the contrary, it suggests that our understanding of the whole process and web are even more important in RD planning and implementation. Neither public (national economic planning commissions) nor private (corporate and business) sector bodies abandon their efforts upon discovering that the factors they deal with are always changing, or because of the inevitable uncertainty. On the contrary, they increase their efforts and so must the case be in RD as well.

For our purposes, the major constraints on RD are grouped into four basic categories. *Resource constraints* (Chapter 2) reflect shortages in natural and/or human resources. The special case of time as an extremely valuable yet relatively scarce natural resource in the development efforts of most countries is included in this section. *Organizational constraints* (Chapter 3) affect RD efforts through their presence both within and between organizations. *Policy constraints* (Chapter 4) are principally the unintended results of well meaning policy interventions, which turn out to have at least as many (and often more) negative effects as positive ones. Such interventions may take place within or outside the RD sphere and have retrogressive effects on rural and agricultural development. Finally, *structural and systemic constraints* (Chapter 5) are identified. These are socio-political boundaries to action and development in all societies, created by and arising out of the essential relationships governing human interaction therein -- the basic rules of the game, so to speak. They are directly concerned with such major issues as the differential access to resources in society, the related distribution of benefits, and the social balance between efficiency and equity.

CHAPTER 2. RESOURCE CONSTRAINTS

Resource constraints are barriers to development erected by the simple unavailability of needed resources. These may be physical, human and/or financial. The deficit may be permanent or temporary, inviolate or redeemable. If at the time of need, however, the required resources are not forthcoming in adequate or threshold quantities, then progress is halted and the constraint may be considered as binding for the moment. In such situations, no amount of ingenuity or application seems to adequately substitute for the lack of the required means.

A. Natural, Human and Financial Resources

Natural resources. Constraints imposed by nature are perhaps the most stark of all, particularly where they constitute non-renewable or very-slowly-renewable resources. The non-availability of land, or land of adequate quality for agricultural production is a representative example. The lack of water, or of suitable climatic conditions are also examples of resource constraints which are hard to shake off, especially in the short run.

Where long-run attempts exist to break such constraints they are often prohibitively expensive and/or require a high level of technical and managerial capability, demands which strain the meager resources of most developing countries (e.g., the land reclamation/anti-desertification efforts in Northern China and Northwestern India, large-scale irrigation projects in most places, schemes in desert areas, etc.). Nature-imposed climatic constraints are perhaps the most immutable (though we shall soon examine the remarkable extent to which man-made constraints are difficult to change). To be sure, substantial recent and current scientific research on agricultural production under "hot-house" conditions, as for instance in growing vegetables in some arid areas of the Middle Eastern states, has shown that nature's constraints can be overcome. But unfortunately, these pilot successes are extremely expensive and would be highly difficult to extend to large-scale agricultural production in resource-poor regions.

Human resources. This constraint can take a number of forms, e.g., the unavailability of production labor, an absence of educated workpower, demographic imbalances and/or mismatches between skilled workers available and skills required. Theoretically, shortages in human resources are much more tractable than comparable shortages in natural ones, even though it still takes time to fill gaps, adjust imbalances, train people, etc. Also, human workpower may be "imported" -- from another region of the country, for instance, or another nation -- but this has its own problems of availability/unavailability, adequacy, and appropriateness, as well as unintended negative side-effects.

Financial resources. Problems in this area are perhaps the most common of the three resource constraints, often functioning as brakes to development even in countries which are in reasonably good shape where physical and human assets are concerned. Examples here are the "newly industrializing countries" of Asia, Africa and Latin America such as Indonesia, Nigeria, Brazil and Mexico. And of course, in those more numerous Third World countries not so well endowed with physical and human resources, financial difficulties add to the burdens already there. Financial problems may be internal or external. On the internal side, taxes never seem to raise enough money to promote the developmental activites so sorely needed, and what little tax monies are raised generally seem to be paid in by the poor through regressive taxation systems, while the rich pay far less than their share.

At the local level, where RD and social forestry activities take place, the problem of financial resource mobilization is especially acute, principally because whatever taxes are to be raised will have to be paid by the better off, for the rural poor really cannot pay much in taxes. And of course the local rich are best able to avoid paying taxes, controlling as they do the very local governments that must impose local tax levies. The result is that local development efforts depend on grants and subsidies from higher level for virtually all their funding.

The situation externally is no better for most states, as is all too painfully evident in the current debt crisis that has sucked even the relatively oil-rich Third World countries like Mexico and Nigeria into its maelstrom, to say nothing of the many states without a petroleum cushion. And the realities of terms of trade and exchange (cheap and volatile raw commodities from the "South" vs. invariably expensive manufactures from the "North") serve mainly to exacerbate the problem. Mobilization of public and private foreign investment, and foreign assistance, are supposed to meet these difficulties but the extent of the effort and the handling of funds somehow does not meet the acknowledged need.

In forestry, as in other developmental areas, these financial exigencies have a real programmatic bite. When resources are scarce, there is competition for them, as economists never tire of telling us. Thus if a forestry program is to get funding (or more funding), some other program, quite likely just as worthy, is necessarily going to get none (or less). And the total sums involved are prodigious. Foley and Barnard (1984: 16) found that over the 1974-84 period, more than 130 farm and community forestry programs had been initiated in 50 countries, involving international donor commitments of more than $US 750 million. In India alone, more than $US 280 million had been commited in the period 1979-84 (ibid., 221), and most of these projects required in-country counterpart funding as well.

Despite these impressive funding levels, few would suggest they are adequate to the task. The World Resources Institute (1985: I, 25), in a recent study sponsored by the World Bank and the United Nations Development Programme, has urged a crash program that would involve some $US 1.9 billion over a five-year period for 32 countries. And to finish the job will likely be even more expensive. South Korea, whose community forestry enterprise is widely regarded as one of the most successful, is reckoned to have spent something like $US 600 million over five years, of which more than 60 percent came from government resources (Arnold, 1983: 188). In the end, quite a number of countries will probably come to match the Korean record.

Obviously the natural, physical and financial resource categories are not mutually exclusive. Most of the time the resource constraints faced by nations, regions, communities and enterprises are a combination of all three, each impinging on and aggravating the others. Examples are almost universal, so common is this joint predicament.

In addition, as touched upon earlier, the constraints have different time-horizons regarding the possibility of resolution. Their varying short-, medium- or long-term characteristics make it difficult to discern their true nature and extent, or gauge their potential consequences at any particular point. Overcoming these hurdles is one of the dilemmas of planning activities for rural development, for it is seldom possible to foresee whether necessary resources and preconditions will be obtained in the right sequence or with the correct timing to achieve a favorable local outcome. Rural institutions help to manage available resources, and to increase their utility and availability to broader constituencies, but unfortunately cannot usually augment the resources themselves, especially from outside sources.

B. The Unique Case of Time as a Special Natural Resource

Everyone involved in the business of economic development wants quick results, whether it is the case of an economic recovery program in an industrialized Western economy, or an agricultural credit/fertilizer project, or a community woodlot/fodder scheme in a developing area. Politicians and civil service officials invariably feel that they have to show strong indications of future success within the first year, followed by demonstrable accomplishment within a couple of years. Forestry planners charged with putting together woodlot schemes, for example, think they will have a much better time of it if they can include in the scheme something like *leucaena leucocephala* that will produce some cuttable fodder within the first year or so. At least *something* must be "delivered" in fairly short order if popular support is to be maintained, a pressing concern indeed in social forestry, where plant protection in the early stages is absolutely vital to project success (see, e.g., the admonitions of Mnzava, 1982 and Kronick,1984).

These pressures are fully understandable. The officials involved in development efforts, whether politicians or administrators, are concerned with matters of great importance to the country (or the district, or village, depending on the scale of the project), matters which directly impinge upon the people's standard of living. Since that standard of living is in all cases considerably lower than acceptable, it is not at all surprising that officials feel themselves under great pressure to do something concrete and fast to improve it. Even if middle and lower level administrators do not find it in themselves to spur things on, their superiors do, so that all up and down the chain of command tenure, promotions and perquisites depend upon discernable results. A government irrigation engineer, for example, needs to show something positive and demonstrable from a new small-scale irrigation project within two or three years at the outside, if he or she is going to advance in the service. Political leaders (whether elected or not) must satisfy a majority of their constituencies and publics in the short term if they are to stay in power, and for them two or three years is a very long time, while five years might as well be forever. Time is a very important matter in the development business.

Success, however, when it comes at all to RD programs, rarely if ever does so in two, three, or even five years. Even when it appears to have done so, there are often deeper, and historically longer-term, explanations. For example, the Green Revolution in the Punjab area of India and Pakistan seems at first glance to have materialized overnight. Over a mere seven-year period in the 1960s the Indian Punjab more than doubled wheat production, while in Pakistan's Punjab the increase was by about two-thirds (Johl and Mudahar, 1974:12; Government of Pakistan, 1980: part II, 26-27).

But though this growth was truly remarkable, it did not at all come about just in a seven-year period. An analysis in only modest depth shows very clearly that the conditions for this achievement had been laid down over the previous 70 years, beginning with the "canal colonies" that were started in the Punjab around the turn of the century (e.g., Raulet, 1976). Similarly, South Korea and Taiwan, both of which had quite phenomenal growth in rice production during the 1950s and 1960s, did not suddenly blossom from moribund backwaters of agricultural stagnation into dynamos of rice output. Each had begun to develop the necessary infrastructure in terms of irrigation, farmer cooperatives and the like under the Japanese back in the 1920s and 1930s (Aqua, 1974 on Korea, and Stavis, 1974 on Taiwan).

Longer time horizons, then, are important and necessary in RD, though perhaps not always the 60-plus years experienced by the Punjab or the 40 and more taken by Korea and Taiwan. Indeed, there is some reason to think that as little as 15 or 20 years might be a sufficient time frame within which to effect real rural change (see Blair, 1982). The point, however, is that even a "mere" 15 years are still a lot longer than most politicians and administrators (or for that matter, officials in the international development community, who have their own careers to get on with, and their own funding constituencies to satisfy) have within their available time horizons.

Fortunately, foresters are accustomed to thinking in terms of longer cycles and so should find this time constraint instinctively less burdensome than their colleagues in the agricultural sector, for whom a 150-day crop can be a very long one indeed!

CHAPTER 3. ORGANIZATIONAL CONSTRAINTS

Most of the constraints involving an implementing organization occur within the structure itself, and are part and parcel of its own nature. However, there are also some constraints that emerge in the linkages that join an organization to its social environment.

A. Within the Organization

Four organizational constraints will be taken up. The first two have proven to be problems in a great many RD programs. The transition from pilot project to full scale effort, and the problem of centralization *vs.* decentralization, both appear to be inherent in the nature of bureaucracy itself, or at least almost inevitably present in RD enterprises. The third theme -- past success as an inhibitor of future change -- is also a common one, though perhaps less serious than the first two. The final intra-organizational constraint concerning the contradiction between regulation and extension is one that affects only some RD efforts but which has a special meaning for forestry.

i. Managing Expansion from Pilot Project to Larger Scale

It makes eminent good sense to begin any large scale activity as an experiment, in order to introduce and test out ideas, and to have the ability to change the design as unforeseen aspects arise (as they always will with any experiment involving human beings), until the model is gradually perfected. Once the "bugs" have been "worked out," it can then be replicated onto a larger scale, e.g., every village in the province, every administrative subdivision in the district, etc.

The problem with this approach is that all too often the pilot project is overly artificial in the sense of being a laboratory; it is a "hothouse" environment in which an experiment may flourish, but only under conditions which are, by their very nature, unlike those of the world outside. Technologically, this is a familiar story in RD. A new variety of rice, for example, is developed at the International Rice Research Institute at

Los Baños in the Philippines that is perhaps two or three times as productive as the traditional varieties that are customarily grown in a country. But these new "miracle rice" strains are bred to grow under comparative laboratory conditions: the best soils, controlled water supply through sprinklers, drainage systems with underground pipes to remove the water from each field exactly on schedule, electric fences around each plot to keep out rodents, precise applications of fertilizers and pesticides, virtually complete weeding, etc. Small wonder, then, that when an LDC farmer attempts to try the new variety on poor soil with bad drainage and uncertain water supply, without proper fertilizer application or enough labor to weed properly, the improvement in yield over the older strains is nothing like what was obtained at Los Baños.

Much the same is true in the organizational sense. Pilot projects in RD tend to be characterized by a number of *artificial conditions* that will not obtain once the project is expanded to full-scale. First, there is the quality of *leadership*. This is the innovative and entrepreneurial spirit that spawns new initiatives in RD and the experiments that prove their worth. People with this spirit mobilize others and inspire them to forget differences and work together in the interest of the project in ways that are not possible later on for expanded versions, when the initial enthusiasm is forgotten. A second factor is the *cadre of field workers* that an inspired leader can attract in the pilot phase. The leader's enthusiasm initially attracts other innovative spirits, but, as the experiment turns into routine with project expansion, enthusiasm begins to flag and the original workers either adapt to routine or leave in search of new challenges.

A third characteristic of the RD pilot project is a *heavy infusion of funds*. The fact that a pilot project exists in the first place, and is viewed as a prototype for a much larger enterprise, necessarily means that important people in the government are sponsoring it and accordingly have a sizeable stake in the project's success. These sponsors most likely have had to argue in governmental councils for their project over others, and this investment of time and effort has given them a real incentive to make it succeed. To increase the chance of success, sponsors will make sure the pilot project has all the resources it needs, particularly funding. Since new projects inevitably run into special problems and develop needs that are often most easily solved with infusions of money, it is clear that the necessary financing is probably going to be fairly sizeable. (We should recall here that sponsors -- both foreign and domestic -- have a special need for speed, and that more money is generally the fastest way to get an apparent solution to pilot project problems, e.g. by hiring more staff, setting up a new division, bringing in an outside consultant, etc.). Needless to say, when programs are in full-scale operation in multiple locations, such lavish extra funding for problem solving is just not available.

Sponsors who provide special funds to ensure success will generally also supply a fourth special factor -- *direct communication between the pilot project in the field and higher levels*, sometimes even at the cabinet or chief-of-state level. Prime Minister Jawaharlal Nehru took direct personal interest in the Community Development Scheme in India in its early phases (Mayer, 1958), as did President Julius Nyerere in the beginning stages of the Ujamaa movement in Tanzania (Fortmann, 1980). This special link means that bureaucratic bottlenecks and slippages are promptly rectified and that intermediary government officials, aware of the high-level patronage, are less likely to interfere. Once the pilot becomes a full-scale program, however, it becomes just another branch of government, and the special channel is lost.

A fifth characteristic often present in laboratory projects is a *willingness to learn from mistakes*, indeed in some cases an insistence on ferreting out problems and failures for their learning value. Such a self-critical attitude is invaluable in the pilot phase and makes a strong contribution to pilot success. But to expect such openness once the project has expanded to full coverage is unrealistic, for those in charge at the later time are career officials who typically have nothing to gain and much to lose from admitting error. As Korten (1980) demonstrates in his "learning process" approach to project management, overcoming these tendencies is not impossible, but it is nevertheless very difficult (see Chapter 7 below).

Sixth, the experimental pilot stage tends to encourage significantly more *participation from below*, both within the project staff and from potential beneficiaries. This is understandable, for at the beginning managers are more amenable to admitting that they don't know exactly what they are doing, and therefore eager to solicit help and advice from whatever quarter they can get it. As programs expand and mature, however, it gradually becomes disadvantageous (and even conterproductive to one's career chances) to admit such failings in front of superiors and subordinates as well as funding donors and recipients.

Finally, there can be and often is a *rigorous monitoring* of every facet of project activity in the pilot phase. Managers wish to move about and see every corner of the project, and they have the time to do so. Account books can be regularly inspected, field work checked, villagers interviewed, and so on. It behooves managers to be seen in the field at this stage, their sleeves rolled up and with their brows covered with sweat.

Later on, however, the rewards come to those engaged in what might be called "normal project management" (after Chambers' (1986) "normal development professionalism") -- tending to office duties, making frequent trips to higher level headquarters, and making sure that the administration goes on smoothly, all activities that run counter to making trips to the field and visiting obscure villages.

The result of all these factors is that when projects grow from pilot to full-scale, enthusiasm evaporates, control atrophies, efficiency withers, corruption flourishes, vested interests move in, and the original purpose gets lost altogether. These negative tendencies are further exacerbated when growth is overrapid. Unfortunately, overrapid expansion is all too common in the RD experience, for, in a situation where most projects do not work very well anyway, when one comes along that looks like it might succeed, there is irresistible pressure from the highest levels to expand it as rapidly as possible. Sadly, where expansion is fastest, so is the potential for detrimental effects setting in the most quickly. Yet on the other hand, it makes little sense to begin a wholly new development effort without some pilot experimentation, and enterprises that cannot be expanded from pilot status to wider level are not going to succeed in any event. Furthermore, if the expansion is too slow, the project is not going to do much for its intended beneficiaries. Two rich illustrations of this metamorphosis from pilot success to project failure (and in at least one of the cases a longer-term reversal to substantial achievement) are the Community Development scheme in India and the Comilla project in Pakistan/Bangladesh, which are explored further in Chapter 9.

ii. Centralization *vs.* Decentralization

The centralization/decentralization constraint to be taken up in this section is if anything even more immutable than the project expansion problem just dealt with above. This is so because, while not every development undertaking warrants a pilot-then-expansion phase, virtually all projects with a field component (i.e., excepting macrolevel activities like "structural adjustment" efforts) finds it necessary to move both ways at the same time. The dilemma thus posed[1] will be the focus of this section, but we should note here that decentralization as a rural development strategy has gained an increasing audience in recent years, and accordingly will be examined in some detail later on in Chapter 7. Here the emphasis will be only on the problem.

Centralization is needed in any organization to enhance accountability, control, and uniformity in the making of decisions. In RD projects in particular, centralization is essential to cut down on corruption, which is usually present in some degree even under the best of circumstances and, unless very carefully and continuously watched, could quickly grow out of control. At the same time, decentralization is needed in all organizations to encourage innovation and initiative. It is especially needed in RD enterprises because of the great variation in local conditions with which project agents must deal in the field. In a word, overcentralized government development efforts simply cannot know what to do in specific situations on the ground.

Problems arise because it is of course necessary for organizations to move in both directions concurrently. And these difficulties are compounded by the fact that movement in either direction does not just merely ignore the contrary one but instead intensifies the problems that the latter is designed to ameliorate. A program emphasizing centralized control, for instance, tends to eliminate scope for local initiative because the overriding concern is for everything to be done in the same way. Imposing order through the center produces uniform behavior in the field (or at least timely and regular project reports from subordinates) and can (though it certainly doesn't always) minimize local corruption, but these dubious achievements generally come at the cost of disappointing field results, because no allowance is taken of local variation. As an illustration, programs designed to deal with middle-sized farms growing rain-fed cash crops such as soybeans are scarcely going to work in villages of small-scale farmers growing irrigated subsistence crops. Any attempt to treat them all similarly, e.g., in a cooperative marketing scheme, is likely to fail.

Even more distressingly, centralization aggravates matters at field level by pressuring local and middle level officials to look only upward in the chain of command. Officials who are out to convince their own superiors that right decisions have been made are not going to waste time worrying about whether those below think things are going well or not, and certainly are not going to bother with the views of the project's intended beneficiaries. Similarly, the next level of supervisors, if only concerned about what *their* bosses think, are not going to spend any more time looking "downwards" in the scale of hierarchy.

On the other hand, if governments decide to decentralize and allow more autonomy to their officers in the field, many of these problems could be solved. Lower level staff would be encouraged to make changes and improvements in projects so as to achieve a better fit with each project site and each local community of beneficiaries; indeed, at least in some cases they could tailor project activities to the needs of individuals, as in a skills training enterprise. The problem, of course, is that those in the field could become too independent and too involved with their publics. To the extent that they can build a "constituency" for the program -- a core of supporters who put political pressure on higher levels to maintain the program -- this kind of involvement may be a good thing. But it can also lead to other and less favorable kinds of involvement, such as corruption or a tendency to steer activities toward those with whom field project staff feel most comfortable, which is to say local elites. To allow decentralization and autonomy, and to give up the benefits of accountability and rigorous monitoring that can only be part of a fairly centralized operation, in other words, is to increase the potential for project-damaging actions and arrangements.

Agricultural credit programs offer an excellent illustration of this dilemma (see Adams et al., 1984; and in the latter volume, Blair, 1984). For a program to even begin to work, agents in the field must be given considerable discretion to decide which farmers or cooperative groups are most viable, which production plans (generally a requirement for obtaining a loan) are most likely to produce a crop, which individuals have the best reputation for good husbandry, etc. But if field agents are given that much discretion, they are in the process also given a large scope for corruption, for they can as easily give the loans to those who give the largest kickbacks as to those who have the best production plans. Needless to say, it is generally the bigger and richer farmers who can give the most kickback money, and so they tend to get most of the loans, thereby depriving the smaller farmers of the money, an outcome particularly ironic in the many programs designed to provide subsidized credit particularly to small and marginal farmers.

The bureaucratic response to this situation is to centralize control of the program, eliminating the discretion that seems so easily to lead to corruption. The method most often used to do this is to require collateral in the form of land for issuing loans, since this is something that can be fairly simply verified through land registry offices. Unfortunately, it also means that loan issue will vary directly with property size -- again, not exactly the ideal outcome in programs intended to include or even emphasize small farmers. Even worse, there is a greater chance of default, because, as is well established, non-repayment in agricultural credit programs varies directly with farm size. Large farmers default more than small ones, principally because they (correctly) estimate that they have the political connections to get away with it. Despite this, officials continue to use land size as a criterion for loans because in a centralized bureaucracy that is the "correct" (i.e., career-promoting) behavior. Money is to be lent to those who pass the "objective" test of having land to pledge as collateral; whether they repay or not is less important. To get involved in the messy details of who is in default and why and what can be done about it is too much for a centralized bureaucracy to deal with (and besides, the individual officers responsible will all have been posted to other jobs by the time that loan overdues have to be declared as defaults). The end result, then, is that programs which had started out to benefit all farmers (or even small farmers exclusively) end up by benefitting mainly the larger ones.

These contradictory needs have their counterpart in the forestry sector, for instance as when Gibbs (1982) notes that on the one hand frequent transfers of officers inhibits any ability to build the personal relationships at local level that would be essential to project success in community forestry, while on the other leaving staff in one place for too long encourages the building of networks for corruption. Resolution of such dilemmas tend to be like that observed in Niger by Brechin and West (1982: 86), who found a "heavy-handed approach" on the part of a highly centralized forestry bureaucracy, which "stifle[d] local level initiative and create[d] general resistance to forestry programs."

In sum, centralization forces tend to be the stronger of the two, at any rate in the shorter run, if only because most project pressures on officials are short-term in nature. But in the end, if an RD project is to succeed in the field, decentralization is virtually a *sine qua non*, which is probably why the topic has attracted a growing interest of late. We will return to this theme in Chapter 7.

iii. Professional Glamour and Past Success

Most professional fields have their more attractive specialties and career paths, and the rural development field is no exception. In agricultural development bureaucracies, "hard" scientific research like crop breeding and toxicology have far more prestige than "softer" realms such as rural sociology and agricultural extension. In general, the time spent in laboratory or office is directly proportional to one's status, while that spent in the field with rural residents is inversely related to it. And if one must go to the countryside, trips should be made in the dry season and contacts should be confined to the better (i.e., richer and more powerful) citizenry (Robert Chambers in his well-written and influential *Rural Development*

[1983] lays out the patterns of "normal development professionalism" most lucidly; see also Chambers, 1986).

This is particularly so when the discipline has enjoyed a history of conspicuous success. Successful general staffs, to take an obvious example, are given to refighting wars they have won. And the results are often far from victorious, as was all too clear in the Anglo-French collapse at the beginning of World War II, or the French and later American military debacles in Indochina in the 1950s and 1960s.

Irrigation engineering offers many examples of a similar pattern in the RD field. Large scale surface water projects such as the Aswan Dam in Egypt, the Gezira scheme in the Sudan, or the Punjab canal project in British India were all hailed as great successes and conferred much prestige on their builders. It is out of such projects that there has come the professional tradition, and with it the pride and *élan* that are so much a part of irrigation engineering today. Unfortunately the professional pride that comes from designing and constructing projects with big dams and command areas of hundreds of thousands (or in some cases millions) of hectares stands in the way of a willingness to work with projects for small tubewells with command areas of 20 hectares or so, even though the latter may well give more irrigated hectarage for the money and be much better suited for particular crops or environments than any massive surface water project. Convincing irrigation engineers to "think small" after they have done well at "thinking big" can be a very hard thing to do.[2] And given the high status that design and construction enjoy as career sectors in the water management field, it can be equally difficult to convince them to devote themselves to the operations and maintenance sectors of their profession, which suffer from a much lower status (see Chambers and Wade, 1980, on this).

Thus large systems are more prestigious than small ones, surface water systems (i.e., those impounding river water in one way or another) rank higher than ground water operations (wells that tap underground aquifers), and design or construction confers more status than operations or maintenance. Now if large-scale, surface water systems and design/construction were the most pressing needs today in the water management sector, this pattern of professional status perception would be highly supportive of the overall RD effort. But in fact the major needs in most LDCs are for smaller systems, ground water exploitation and managing and rehabilitating the large systems already in place rather than building new ones.

As if to aggravate an already difficult situation, intertwined throughout these issues of scale, source (of water) and sector is the whole matter of corruption. Simply put, the opportunities for bribes, kickbacks, invoicing manipulations and the like are far greater with large-scale, surface water design and construction activities than is the case with their opposites; small scale, ground water operations and maintenance are not entirely bereft of possibilities for illegal gratification, but, by comparison with the more prestigious branches of the field, their potential is very modest.

Forestry has similar problems. Managing large production forest tracts (especially in the parastatal forest development corporations that have become more common in recent decades) ranks higher than social forestry by a considerable margin. And mensuration or species development for production forestry has more prestige than conducting trials for fuelwood trees. Finally, the potential for venality is much greater in production forestry where large lots are sold off to substantial bidders than in laying out and supervising village woodlots. As in water management, if the major needs in LDCs were for production forestry and conservation, these attitudes would be quite advantageous for maximizing sustained yield (provided the corruption could be kept from getting out of hand), but here too the actual mix of needs are rather different from what the profession is currently oriented toward. Production forestry and conservation will continue to be important, no doubt, but equally pressing needs (indeed perhaps more pressing in view of the failure of forest protection efforts in so many areas) exist in social forestry, that is in those areas of the field that are so far the least statusful and rewarding.

In order to become effective in reaching farmers and improving water distribution and use, irrigation engineers have had to reconsider priorities and redirect energies, in effect to reorient much of their professional approach, an experience that has much to say to professionals in the forestry field. Forestry has a similar challenge in the LDCs, but the profession has been faced with what amounted to an equally daunting challenge in the advanced countries over the past two decades in the form of the environmental movement, which has assaulted the very fundaments of the profession (as, e.g., Kennedy, 1985, shows in the American case; see also Buttel and Flinn, 1974), and has managed for the most part to come to terms with it. Both the irrigation example and the potential for reorienting development administration in general will be pursued further in Chapters 6 and 7.

iv. Regulation *vs*. Promotion

This constraint is a bit like the centralization *vs* . decentralization dilemma in that only one or the other can be fruitfully pursued at one time, yet the dictates of the development process are such that both need to be pursued simultaneously. The problem has become a familiar one to forestry in recent years. Organizations that have traditionally served to protect forests now find themselves called upon to become extension agencies preaching forestry involvement to the very same people that they had earlier been trying to keep separated from the trees. Those who were policemen are now expected to become salesmen.

Such a combination of roles is difficult, to say the least, and it is not surprising that the policeman tends to predominate over the salesman when there is conflict between the two roles, either in a department as a whole or within the breast of an individual forester. All too often forestry staff have "promoted" social forestry endeavors like woodlot projects by acting as though villagers were a rather undisciplined army that had to be firmly mobilized into action and told what to do (Bogach, 1985: 57-65, describes the patterns well). Needless to say, failures under such rigid top-down management approaches have been frequent. Niger (Brechin and West, 1982), Senegal (Freeman and Resch, 1985/6), India (Commander, 1986) and Nepal (Arnold and Campbell, 1986) all offer evidence of how hard it is to give up the policeman's role.

In a very real sense, the history of the whole RD experience in the last 30 years is in many ways just such an attempt to graft an advocacy role into a traditional police mission.[3] The difference, in this connection, between forestry and RD as a whole is that today forestry is a single sector wrestling with the problem, whereas in RD it has been the entire panoply of organizations involved in administering the countryside that have faced this issue. In colonial Africa and Asia in the earlier part of this century the major function of rural administration was to preserve law and order and to collect taxes. Various development ideas were thought up from time to time, but these were the exceptions (often the brainchildren of individual and -- by the standards of their services and times -- clearly eccentric administrators), not the norm. "Development" consisted of building up a few extractive mineral industries or perhaps some plantation export crop operations, but it was not on the colonial agenda as an overarching goal of government that would affect the broad mass of people.

With independence and new national ambitions for improving the standard of living and quality of life, rural administration was given the task of rural development, in addition to its policing and taxing duties. The transition was not an easy one, particularly for officers who had come up in a service where the rewards, promotions and recognition were not slanted towards development but for fulfilling the older mission. It is only gradually that rural administration in several places has responded to these new demands through such means as building extension services in agronomy, animal husbandry, public health, etc., and the experience has not been easy. This last constraint, then, is one that can be overcome, but only with a great deal of planning and work. The theme of institutional change is explored more fully in Chapter 7.

B. Linkages Between Organization and Environment

As has been indicated at some length in the previous sections, many of the constraints facing RD organizations are to be found within the organizations themselves. However, there are a number of others that exist in the relationship between organizations and their social environment. To survive over time, any agency must somehow fill needs felt by others outside itself. An organization must build constituencies or publics that have a strong interest in seeing it continue, and which have the political voice to ensure that their interests are realized. For example, a public works department must build and maintain roads in such a way that a significant number of people who have some political say in public affairs want the department to stay in business, to keep building roads and to continue maintaining the road network.

This need to build constituencies was much smaller in earlier times when rural people by and large did not matter so much to colonial governments. So long as nothing of consequence to the colonial power (such as insurrection or widespread riots) happened in the countryside, which was most of the time, rural areas could be and were ignored. Rural people other than a few big landholders were not really citizens; they did not count. Today, to be sure, vast inequalities and inequities remain in the countryside, but in a real way rural masses do count, in some countries because they vote, in others because they may cause unrest if not attended to, but always because they must have a role if there is to be any serious development outside the urban industrial sector.

Accordingly, RD organizations need to build linkages to those who use their services, for two reasons. The more obvious one is that there must be somebody to use a service in order for it to be provided for any length of time. The other reason is a bit more subtle but is nonetheless real. For a service-providing agency to endure, there must be somebody not only to use its service but also somebody to demand it. This is true especially if there is a threat to the providing agency, whether it be in the form of a budget cut, altered macrolevel priorities or waning donor enthusiasms. Agencies that do not have constituencies do not last. Today, for instance, there would be a hue and cry from farmers' groups in many LDCs if agricultural extension services were withdrawn; it would erupt because of the linkages such services have built up over the years with their clients. And it is precisely because such a hue and cry *would* erupt in these countries that the extension services are kept in place even in times of budgetary stringency.

The lack of such a constituency or support base, then, can be a very severe constraint on an organization, both in terms of budget allocations and survival itself. By remaining in effect off in the periphery with only timber cutters and processors for constituencies, forestry found itself with few friends when the environmental movement began to make new demands on it. Without a vocal constituency that wants it to go on, social forestry will not deserve to last very long.

C. Ignoring Indigenous Rural Knowledge and Priorities

Answering as they do their professional callings, rural development professionals look for standards, guidance, innovation and understanding to their Western-oriented disciplines. What is worth knowing and implementing is what has been developed at the laboratories of Oxford or the University of California at Davis, not what local farmers know. More recently the radius of origin for acceptable wisdom has enlarged to include what has emerged from scientific research at such places as the International Rice Research Institute (IRRI) in the Philippines at Los Baños, or the International Institute of Tropical Agriculture (IITA) in Nigeria at Ibadan, and in some countries the national agricultural research structure as well (as with the agricultural universities in India, some of which enjoy world-class reputations for their research). But Los Baños, Ibadan and even such institutes as the agricultural university at Ludhiana in India are still a very long way from farmers' fields. Yet it is places such as these that tend to be seen as the sole sources of the knowledge that is to be deployed to promote agricultural development.

That RD professionals should look upward and outward for what they feel they should know is not difficult to understand when one reflects that the history of agriculture in the West for the past hundred years and more has been one of steady technological upgrading, of "shifting the production function upward" through improvement of cultivation technology, almost all of which has been developed at places like Oxford and Davis. The fact that in the West the relevance of scientific research in agriculture and the effectiveness of extension work to spread research results has depended crucially on what farmers have been concerned with and have wanted to know seems somehow to get lost in the justified admiration that has been showered on the Western research establishment.

Unfortunately international donors and Third World adminstrators tend to think that only outside, "higher" knowledge is relevant to the development enterprise. When this attitude is combined with the traditional disdain that urban-based literate professionals have traditionally had for rural, illiterate peasants, the result is a resolute refusal to believe that intended project beneficiaries know anything worth listening to.[4] The fact that "rural people's knowledge" in Robert Chambers' (1983) phrase (or "indigenous technical knowledge;" see Chambers and Jiggins, 1987) is the outcome of countless years of experimentation and that peasant farmers are constantly conducting micro-trials of new ideas in their husbandry is generally ignored altogether in the RD business (indeed, such experimentation gets interpreted as deviance by those who do not follow the recommended practices; see Chambers and Jiggins, 1987: 115). And there is little chance that administrators and researchers will discover this rich store of rural people's knowledge, given their antipathy toward spending any time in the field. The sort of "rural development tourism" (another Chambers' phrase from his 1983 work) generally practiced -- confined to the dry season, paved roads, and "model farmer" informants -- will scarcely yield much of value except for reports to be sent upwards through the RD chain of command.

The consequences of such attitudes for agricultural development are severe. RD agents and managers have little idea of what farmers actually know or do, and so have little notion of what they need to know in order to improve production. Not surprisingly, much of what is suggested to farmers is irrelevant and even wrong. There is little if any feedback from the intended "consumers" of the research back to the researchers, with the result that the latter have no idea of whether their new technologies are workable or not under actual field conditions. To some extent, farmers get by with their own "applied research" in spite of the indifference from the official establishment (see, e.g., Brammer's 1980 Bangladesh case study), but clearly the RD process would move much more satisfactorily if there were effective ties between research establishment, administrators and farmers, kept operative through a mutual respect between the three groups.

Parallels abound in forestry, which likewise has an international base firmly established at places like the Oxford Forestry Institute and the Forestry Department at the University of California's Berkeley campus. "Rural people's knowledge" is extensive, as for example Montagne (1985/6) shows in his study of indigenous silviculture in Niger and Mali. Chambers (1983) cites a study by David Brokensha and Bernard Riley, who found Kenyan foresters convinced that Mbeere villagers did not know how to germinate seeds for the locally prized *mukau* tree. Actually, as the villagers knew quite well, germination took place when goats ate the tree's fruit and then passed the seeds in their droppings. Chambers' observation on this is worth repeating at some length:

> The germination of the mukau tree combines the low status of the indigenous trees, the low status of the goat, and the even lower status of goats' droppings. It is no wonder that they pass unnoticed and their potential is overlooked: a programme to germinate mukau trees, however admirable a long-term investment for the people of Mbeere, would require foresters to collect the seeds of an indigenous tree, keep goats, feed the seeds to the goats, collect the goats' droppings, and then tend the droppings with care. (Chambers, 1983: 82).

Foresters (and project planners) also tend to think that, because they know what is best ecologically on a large scale and what the macro-economy most needs in the way of forestry products, they should decide what local people must do to preserve the environment and meet macroeconomic needs. The local people themselves, in this view, need only to be mobilized into action and given orders. The thought that those who are to do the work should be consulted about what they want is not considered.

Fuelwood projects are an excellent case in point here. In many African areas such efforts have failed, principally because fuelwood is commercially feasible only when it can be gathered as a free good (generally from public lands) to be sold. If commercially valuable land is to be used, the "opportunity cost" (i.e., the sacrifice made by not using the land for other purposes) becomes too high, and the projects fail. Thus as Foley reports, the $US 160 million spent on fuelwood plantations in the African Sahel between 1975 and 1982 ended "with very little indeed to show for it" (Foley, 1986: 69; see also O'Keefe et al., 1986: 77; and more generally Arnold, 1983: 184). India presents a similar story, where fuelwood projects have met production targets but failed to fulfill their purpose, because villagers did not use or sell the wood for fuel, but rather marketed it as higher-priced construction poles and pulpwood (Blair, 1986).

---

[1]There are a number of treatments of this dilemma in the literature. See for example, Bryant and White (1982: ch. 8).

[2]It should be noted that "thinking small" does not mean necessarily thinking simply, for tubewell systems can be just as intellectually challenging and technologically complex as large surface water schemes.

[3]There is a substantial literature on this transition, mostly from the 1960s, when the change was in the process of taking place. See Braibanti, 1969; LaPalombara, 1963; Raphaeli, 1968. All of these are edited collections of essays many of which deal with this topic.

[4]In addition to the work by Chambers and Jiggins cited in this section, see Bryant and White's (1982: 179-203) analysis on lower-level RD administrators' views of the public, and more generally Norgaard's 1984 analysis. All are rich in insights relevant to forestry.

CHAPTER 4. POLICY CONSTRAINTS

Policies intended to accomplish specific goals, or assist particular activities, almost invariably have side-effects on other sectors, many of which can be quite detrimental. Oftentimes these drawbacks come about through misunderstanding or inadvertence, as for example, when agricultural officials in India urged price support policies in the 1970s to encourage farmers to grow more foodgrains in order to take advantage of the new high yielding varieties (HYVs). These policies did indeed work in the sense that a great deal more foodgrain was produced. However, this success came about to a considerable extent through substituting foodgrains for pulses, as farmers shifted from the one crop to the other as yields and profit opportunities began to appear more promising with foodgrains. This pattern caused a serious nutritional problem, in that pulses had traditionally supplied the critical amino acid (lysine) that is lacking in wheat and rice, and which is needed to give a balanced protein component to the vegetarian diet of most Indians. The planners therefore improved the nutritional situation on the calorie front in terms of total foodgrains produced, but they did so at the expense of the protein position (for more explanation, see *inter alia*, Cassen, 1975; for a more general consideration of the problem, Cerescope, 1983).

This example is one of misguided policy or perhaps of unanticipated outcome.[1] More commonly, though, policy constraints stem not so much from inadvertence as from the nature of the socio-economic and political milieu within which policy must be made and executed. To take another dietary case, in Brazil during the 1970s, when the country desperately needed foreign exchange in order to pay the huge import bills it was running up, especially for petroleum products, it found that one way to earn foreign exchange was to export cash crops, in particular soybeans. By subsidizing soybeans Brazil soon became the world's number two exporter for that product, but a part of the cost was that land was taken out of production from black beans, which serve the same nutritional function in Brazil as do pulses in India, i.e., they supply the missing lysine to the rice or maize diet that is the staple of the lower income groups. Here the cause was not so much inadvertence as the government's calculated choice to raise foreign exchange needed to pay import bills (Pastore, 1977; Knight, 1979). More recently, also in Brazil, the drive to grow alcohol-producing crops to make fuel for powering vehicles has had much the same effect in making scarce black beans more expensive (Gray, 1982). There are numerous other examples of this as well, for instance Franke and Chasin (1980) on the Sahel.

Going the other way in holding down prices to protect consumers also has its pitfalls, as became evident in Mexico recently when the government kept the prices of the main staple maize crop intentionally low, only to see farmers switch to sorghum, which was not controlled, but neither is it eaten by humans in Mexico (Walsh, 1985).

Whether due to misjudgments, design or the effects of political economy, policy constraints on welfare and development can be quite severe, and an appreciation of them can help planners and implementors deal with, perhaps even attenuate, their impact. There are several kinds of policy constraints.

A. Policies Favoring Urban Over Rural Interests

One interpretation of the process of economic development focuses on the adjustment in relative shares of agricultural and non-agricultural (manufacturing) activities in society. Historically, the ratios of both investment and employment in agriculture to investment and employment in non-agricultural activities have fallen as development has occurred, especially in capitalist economies. Since this is a relative shift in resources, the absolute amounts of one or the other can and do rise at particular times without interfering with the overall change in emphasis.

This aspect of structural change in developing economies has become enshrined in theoretical and planning approaches. It is argued that while agriculture is by far the largest sector in economies of less developed countries, it is often also less efficient and slower growing. This poses an obvious problem for the maximization of economic surplus necessary for capital formation and future growth. If the best use is to be made of available resources, then either agriculture's productivity would have to be raised to at least match, if not actually surpass, that of manufacturing, or alternatively resources would need to be transferred out of the less efficient sector (agriculture) to the more efficient one (industry). The initial response was to choose only the latter course, though later it was decided that a blend of the two would obviously be the most appropriate. Nevertheless, for a number of powerful theoretical, ideological and practical reasons, the actual stress has for long been on moving resources out of agriculture and into manufacturing (see Johnstone and Kilby 1979; Mellor 1966, 1976).

In most societies there exist a very large number of possible interactions between the agricultural and non-agricultural sectors. At the broadest and most general level we can identify the demand from the agricultural sector for manufactured goods of all kinds as one important relationship. Similarly and conversely, there is the large industrial requirement for what are termed agricultural wages goods, or basic food products essential for the dietary welfare of manufacturing workers.

The interrelationship can also be expressed in terms of visible and invisible transfers from and to agriculture. Visible transfers from agriculture take the form of taxes, voluntary savings, rent, interest, and other payments emanating from farm households which go for non-agricultural purposes. In the reverse direction are subsidies received by the agricultural sector for various inputs used by it, government investments in rural infrastructure and in agricultural research and development, private investment, loans and other financial receipts from the non-farm sector, and non-farm generated agricultural income, to name an important few.

Invisible transfers are those associated with changes in the average price of non-agricultural products purchased by farm households relative to the average price of goods they sell to the other sector. This relationship is commonly referred to as the terms of trade between agriculture and industry, and the transfer of resources from the operation of this mechanism can be very large. Often, as noted above, a determination of the terms of trade for agriculture arises out of conscious policy. But in addition, it also occurs as the unintended result of changes in agricultural and industrial productivity. It may further result from non-agricultural price policy, e.g., exchange controls, product controls, and currency overvaluation.

In theory, temporarily adverse terms of trade for agriculture are intended to lead to a higher standard of living for all, including the agricultural sector. A reduction of agricultural prices relative to industrial prices is in effect a real income transfer for the urban labor force. Business is enabled to preserve a lower wage structure, and thus increase profits and accumulation. Greater profits mean higher levels of capital formation and productive investment in all goods and services, industrial as well as agricultural. Agriculture's adversity is therefore relative, not absolute, and ideally temporary. Such is the theory at any rate.

In reality, many problems arise. The enormously complex inter-sectoral relationship makes it exceedingly difficult to plan accurate policies for these transfers. For instance, insufficient flow out of agriculture would inhibit growth in the rest of the economy. Too dominant an agricultural sector, if it leads to upward pressures on food prices (especially those of wages goods) could not only inhibit industrial profits (by making foodstuffs more expensive and thus forcing industries to pay their workers more) but also might well lead to urban mass discontent and even government destabilization. One need only recall relatively recent food riots in Egypt and Poland after government attempts to raise food prices, as well as the abrupt policy reversals in both cases once the riots had turned serious -- to realize that goverments are generally very sensitive indeed to such matters. On the other hand, if the terms of trade were to go too far in favor of industry, it would depress agricultural prices, and so production as well, with the result that food supplies would become chronically short, as has happened in a number of countries as well.

There are other pitfalls also. Even if policies could be devised and implemented for precise transfers between sectors, those transfers going from agriculture to industry must be put to productive use in the latter sector for the total economy to benefit. But all too often this does not happen. The private manufacturing sector sometimes chooses to adjust for additional domestic demand through ways other than increasing output, for example through imports. Or it may invest in speculative areas like real estate or foreign exchange that are not conducive to the national welfare. Nor are all the abuses in the private sector. Public-sector manufacturing operations often allocate too much resources to prestige schemes (e.g., steel industries or heavy electricals) which are not the best investments, or governments "divert" the funds to social schemes. Thus the feedback loops to agriculture are not completed (i.e., it does not benefit from the increased goods and services produced by the industrial sector) and in effect it is debilitated to no real purpose.

In addition to these factors and influences, there are others which lead to urban interests being better served than rural ones. Questions of power, privilege and class have a say here, often connected to the ability to organize compact urban masses more easily and effectively than thinly spread rural populations, for support or protest (which is in part why the food riots mentioned above occurred so quickly and with such effect). For these and other reasons, we find a great imbalance between city and country as we look around most of the world -- with the latter epitomizing poverty and the former comparative well-being.

This gap has been termed the "urban bias" (Lipton, 1977) and principally ascribed to an uneven conflict between rural and urban classes which the latter invariably win. This is "the most important class conflict in the poor countries of the world today," according to Lipton, more important than that between labor and capital, or foreign and national interests. "Urban bias" is a state of mind of government officials, consultants, planners and other policy makers, and is manifested in the (mis)allocation of investment resources affecting income, welfare, type and location of industry, agricultural production, etc. It causes such apparently enigmatic situations as starvation in LDCs which are principally rural and which produce enough grain to be able to actually export it, and malnutrition in affluent communities in the West which produce but apparently are not able to properly distribute most of the necessities of life.

That there is an urban-bias operating would not be questioned by most. Yet the theory of rural poverty as expounded by "urban-bias" analysts appears inadequate at best and retrogressive at worst. Inadequate because while it describes urban bias, it does not explain its causes or roots in any systematic way. Geography is substituted for production, attitudes for socio-historical processes, and social psychology for political economy. Indeed, the theory is even retrogressive because some of the arguably more basic causes which lead to urban and other biases are overturned or discounted, all of which would need to be analyzed and addressed to achieve adequate redress.

Perhaps a more searching analysis is attempted by Pierre Spitz (1978) in a paper in which he, like Lipton, seeks to understand why the people who work on the land are the first to suffer from famine. Spitz also identifies "the power relations between the urban population and the rural population" as one of the main explanatory factors, but he prods deeper to seek the root, not being satisfied with the level at which the urban-bias explanation operates. He places this rural-urban inequality in the larger context of other negative social forces, including inequities within and between nations, and most importantly, inequalities which prevail within the rural areas themselves.

To sum up, urban bias is an undeniable social phenomenon, therefore it needs to be squarely faced if problems of inequity are to be tackled. But to face it properly one needs to go beyond the apparent surface bias, which is after all only a symptom of a deeper social malaise, and search for the stronger forces of imbalance and disparity which govern regressive production relations. The latter produce not only "urban" biases but also those of income, as we have noted, and region, as we will shortly see.

The effects of "urban bias" would seem *a priori* to be less obvious in the forestry sector, but nonetheless may be very real. One example might be governmental encouragement, either direct or indirect, of charcoal consumption in the cities without any concomitant effort to promote greater or more efficient production in the countryside. This could result in wasteful amounts of fuelwood resources being used for making charcoal, as well as rural consumers losing out to their more privileged urban counterparts in the heightened competition for fuel. In a number of African countries, for instance, wood makes up the key industrial fuel. for example, it is estimated to provide some 64 percent of Kenya's industrial needs, and fully 88 percent of Tanzania's (Barnard and Zaror, 1986: 78). Thus any effort to increase industrialization in Kenya or Tanzania will in all probability also increase the process of deforestation, or just as bad, by enlarging the commercial demand for wood, take it away from those (mostly women) who had used it as a free commodity and turn it over to those (mostly men) who would sell it in the now brisker market (Foley, 1986: 68).

A second example is the pattern that appears to have emerged in parts of India in which state governments encourage and subsidize eucalyptus pulpwood plantations on land that had been used for foodcrops. This initiative produces more feedstock for the growing paper industry and enables (mostly urban) consumers to have more paper, but does little for the countryside, which sees a reduced demand for labor and finds trees that have little use for fodder (animals don't like it) or fuelwood (the species used in India mostly don't burn well for cooking). In the view of Shiva and her colleagues (1982, 1987) who have studied this situation at some length, what is happening here is basically urban purchasing power sucking forest resources out of the countryside.

B. Policies Concentrating Rather than Redistributing Income

The history of rural development is littered with examples of policies originally designed to assist all sections of the rural communities, or even to focus benefits particularly on lower income strata, but which in practice resulted in concentrating income gains toward the rich. Much of the "community development" strategies of the 1950s and early 1960s, for example, were premised on the idea of an economically homogeneous countryside, or in effect a classless peasantry. Projects that would meet the "felt needs" that were expressed by a community's "natural leaders" (to use the phrasing then in vogue) would, it was felt, be good for the entire community. Thus schools, or animal husbandry extension systems, or farm-to-market roads, would benefit all equally. The archetypal program here was the Indian Community Development effort, which began in 1949 in one administrative block of around 100,000 population and by 1963 had covered all the 5000 blocks in the entire country.

Today it stretches the bounds of credibility to accept that those directing the program had no idea that Indian villages were anything but homogeneous entities -- a breathtaking *naïveté* by any standards -- but that conception of rural reality nevertheless apparently did pass for social science wisdom at the time (Blair, 1982: 80-102). As has been well documented (e.g., Myrdal, 1968: 887-891, 1339-1346; Bendix 1969: 338-356), the program in fact did not distribute its benefits equally to all in a classless countryside, but instead funneled its largesse to the already privileged elements. It is not the poor, after all, who can afford to send their children to newly available schools (rather than putting them to work as soon as possible), or who possess draft animals to be inoculated in pilot schemes, or who have crop surpluses to haul to market over newly constructed roads.

Fortunately, not all RD schemes have been so relatively unsophisticated. Other programs have been more discriminating in concept and design, taking into account rural differentiation and the separation of people into classes or strata. However, having done that, many efforts still frankly aimed to benefit the richer landowning classes initially, hoping to later indirectly also benefit the poor, through some sort of "trickle-down" effect. This kind of employment generation rationale, characteristic of some development projects in the "growth with equity" era of the 1970s, was undeniably an advance over earlier assumptions about homogeneous peasant societies, but nonetheless proved to be almost as futile.

Many, perhaps even most, RD projects of this genre did indeed provide a modicum of material benefits to the poor, but this strained "trickle-down" was in the end almost always accompanied by a much more massive "flow-up" mechanism which siphoned income from the poor to better endowed groups. To use an example from irrigation, first there might be an increased demand for labor from bigger landholders benefited by an irrigation scheme, which would indeed provide some additional income to the landless poor, but then consequent rising real wages would soon lead to the deployment of more family labor by landowners on the one hand, and to partial mechanization on the other. The result after a few years could very well be greatly increased crop production, substantially enhanced rural wealth, and yet little if any reduction of rural poverty.

Still other RD policies endeavor to focus directly on the rural poor, such as the small farmer credit programs that we have mentioned in several places. Sadly, these also inexorably seem to channel advantages to the already rich. Similarly, rural works programs appear to benefit the rural privileged. The idea here is to aid the poor directly by mobilizing large numbers of poor people in labor-intensive schemes like road building, canal repair and construction, etc. The money the workers receive allows them to buy food (sometimes, if schemes can be properly coordinated, the very food produced through irrigation projects of the sort mentioned above) thereby marrying effective demand with increased supply. At other times the marriage is "arranged", as it were, as part of the project itself in the form of "food for work" efforts, in which foodgrains are directly given to project workers in lieu of a cash wage (a practice which has the additionally beneficial effect of insulating workers against sudden swings in local food prices).

There exist cases where such rural works schemes have been quite successful in channeling income to the rural poor, e.g., the Employment Guarantee Scheme in the state of Maharashtra in India over the last several years (Government of India, 1980; Reynolds and Sundar, 1977).[2] Far more typically, however, local political elites get control of the rural works activity, a large part of the money never reaches the village level, and workers that actually do get hired get paid considerably less than the "guaranteed" rate, with the rest of their intended compensation being skimmed off by the local power elites (see, e.g., Thomas and Hook, 1977).

Forestry is scarcely immune to these tendencies. One instance is the World Bank-sponsored PICOP (the acronym is for the Paper Industries Corporation of the Philippines) project for growing pulpwood. Although successful in a number of ways, one of its more serious shortcomings was a failure to reach the poorest members of its target community (Hyman, 1983). An example from India comes from the Gujarat community forestry experience analyzed in Chapter 1, where one of the cautionary tales that emerged was that the program in its earlier years exhibited a definite big farmer bias. In its initial four years, almost three-fifths of the free seedlings distributed for farm forestry went to landholders with more than two hectares (about 28 percent of the households participating in the project). As one study done within the state forestry department observed:

> There is no denying the fact that initially big farmers were in the forefront to grab the advantage of free distribution of seedlings, but this could be explained by the fact that for adoption of the innovative ideas of a change from traditional

practices, it is always the big and well-to-do farmers, who could afford to take financial risks, and active interest in innovations and changes (Java, 1985: 141).

As the quotation indicates, to be aware of these tendencies is not *ipso facto* to be able to control them. To take the rural works example, funds intended to provide wages do not get diverted to people of rural influence just because of administrative inefficiency. They generally get diverted as part of that political pattern that ties together village and national elites, as part of the linkage of political patronage that holds so many LDCs together. This general topic will be taken up in more detail below in Chapter 5.

C. Policies Displacing Labor

A very large portion of international development efforts of the 1970s were concerned with employment creation. Indeed, the "growth with redistribution" strategies of that decade would have been impossible without a strong emphasis on creation of jobs (e.g., Chenery et al., 1974 and 1979). Bettering the lot of the rural poor was predicated upon providing them with adequate purchasing power, and this meant generating employment. A number of government policies were devised to accomplish this, both short- and long-term. Not all, however, were successful, and many had the reverse effect of displacing labor, even though the intent was to increase employment.

The "Green Revolution" of the late 1960s and early 1970s offers a good illustration. In many ways it was an ideal advance for Third World agriculture, for not only did it create jobs, but in the process it also produced the very "wages goods" most needed by the poor in the form of foodgrains. This development thus potentially solved the old problem of new rural employment leading to inflation as increased wages available compete for an unchanged quantity of foodstuffs. The rural poor, it was hoped, would be hired to grow additional food, and a part of the additional product could then be available to them to consume against their new and/or higher wages.

The Green Revolution offered such a possibility in two ways (Brown, 1970). First, plant geneticists at centers like CIMMYT (el Centro Internacional de Mejormiento de Maíz y Trigo) in Mexico and IRRI (the International Rice Research Institute) in the Philippines bred new varieties of foodgrains that were shorter and had thicker, sturdier stalks, enabling the plants to respond to increased applications of fertilizer and water without collapsing ("lodging") under their own weight. Farmers could as a result greatly increase production through the use of more nutrients and water. Also, more labor was needed for all the activities of the agricultural process: ploughing, seeding, transplanting (for paddy rice), applying fertilizer and pesticides (HYV's tended to be more vulnerable to pests and diseases than traditional strains), irrigating, weeding, harvesting, processing, storing and transporting to market.

Second, the new HYVs were photoinsensitive, with shorter growing periods. They took less time to mature (for instance, 120 days instead of 160 for some new rice strains), and did not depend on seasonal changes in the length of the day for their "instructions" on when to flower, when to seed, etc. With shorter growing sessions and independence from seasonality, many farmers could now grow two crops a year instead of one, thereby doubling their demand for labor.

Demand for labor, accordingly, did go up with the Green Revolution. Government policies, however, did not always facilitate such trends, and in some cases even counteracted them. In Pakistan, for instance, as the HYVs came into widespread use, the government began to offer substantial subsidies for the import of tractors, thereby encouraging landowners to substitute mechanical for labor power (Gotsch, 1973). Additionally, in many countries generous subsidies on inputs served to misallocate them in directions that did not maximize labor utilization or crop production. This happened because the subsidies, by reducing the cost of inputs below market price, tended to subject them to allocation through bribe, kickback and political influence.

As always, it was the bigger, richer and less efficient farmers that were best able to mobilize such extralegal resources. They secured most of the inputs, even though small farmers would arguably have made better use of them, both in terms of employment as well as output expansion. Removing the subsidies would have allocated the inputs by market price, forcing purchasers to derive maximum return from them -- a condition that would in turn have meant more labor utilization.[3] However, this would have been hard to do, for the reasons elaborated in Chapter 5 below.

Other well-intentioned policies have had similar negative results, although in a somewhat more indirect fashion. By increasing food prices, for example, (i.e., the government procurement price for foodgrains) in order to induce farmers to grow more food, governments have in some cases also led them to evict their tenants and sharecroppers, so that they could resume cultivation of less productive land that had been marginal when food prices were low but which became valuable when prices went up. In other cases, rising food prices led to greater production, but also a decreased demand for labor, as rising real wages drove farmers to replace hired labor with family labor. Here total labor utilization went up, but the number of days worked by landless laborers may actually have gone down. Increasing prices without providing job security, in short, may have resulted in both more food and more unemployment.

None of this should be taken to mean that the development of new agricultural technologies was itself a mistake. Any innovation that pushes up food production significantly is an improvement, and needs to be undertaken. However, the point does remain that more awareness might have made it possible to forestall potential negative side effects, particularly those that injured precisely those constituencies that were supposed to benefit most from the innovation.

Some of the detrimental effects would of course have been more difficult to prevent than others, for example, the loss of jobs for landless laborers when family labor was mobilized. On the other hand it probably would have been possible to do something more to protect the rights of sharecroppers against eviction, or to adjust some of the subsidies on inputs that biased their distribution toward richer farmers who used them less labor intensively. To complicate matters further, the barriers to remedial action were not only those of ignorance or uncertainty, caused by a novel situation. Even if the dimensions of the problem and the path to the solution had been clear, it would have been difficult to prevent a large share of its rewards from goig to big farmers, for they constitute a powerful constituency that is difficult to bypass. Nevertheless, it is clear that much more attention could have been devoted to anticipating and ameliorating the Green Revolution's effects on labor.

The Green Revolution is but one illustration of the labor displacement problem. Other examples abound, such as the replacement of subsistence crops with cattle and/or cotton production for export in Central America, and the introduction of cash crops in a number of West African countries, particularly in the Sahel. Some of these cases will be dealt with later, but here we note that these problems of labor displacement should also be of particular concern for forestry, particularly in farm forestry and/or agroforestry enterprises, where trees replacing foodcrops may well bring down the local demand for labor (Foley and Barnard, 1984: 93-94). For example, governments may wish or be constrained to encourage farmers to grow fuelwood, pulpwood or fodder on their own land, even at the cost of some crop displacement. But if, as is likely judging from experience, a principal motivation of farmers switching to such farm forestry is a reduction in their labor bill, workers are going to be thrown out of jobs. A government may finally decide that even such a tradeoff is worth it, but at the very least this should be the result of a careful weighing of costs and benefits and not something that just happens by default. If, as may well be the case, costs are mostly borne by the poor, and gains reaped by the rich, there would be a strong case for modifying or even dropping the project.

D. Policies Favoring the "External" Over the "Internal"

Very often there is the surface hum of development in a region but no benefit accruing to anyone locally. This occurs when external interests with designs to exploit local natural or human resources enter the area, sometimes clearly temporarily. While the exploitation is in progress, there are nominal signs of growth and development. But because the investment is from outside the region, the returns also for the most part leave the area. There is seldom local reinvestment or long-term benefit.

Unfortunately, many development plans and programs fall into this pattern almost without noticing it or evincing concern. Export crop programs often belong to this category, as do "export platforms" utilizing cheap labor for high technology industries in some cases, and such extractive industries as mining and forestry. The extractive sector is especially egregious in this regard where there is little or no in-country processing before export (e.g., when ore is shipped directly abroad for refining or logs are sent away even for rough sawmilling), for it is in the processing that much more value-added is created than in the extracting itself, as mining engineeers and foresters know all too well. This idea is one of the central themes of the section on regional and area development, and is explored more fully in Chapter 8.

E. Equity and Efficiency in Development Policy

Ever since the late 1940s and early 1950s, when the study of development once again became an accepted part of mainstream economic inquiry after a break of almost three-quarters of a century, the issue of efficiency *vs.* equity has assumed an important position in theoretical arguments as well as in practical planning. Sometimes presented as a tradeoff between the poles of growth and equity, the issue has been under constant discussion, and professional opinion has swung approximately twice so far between the two.

The efficiency/growth *vs.* equity pendulum began in efficiency's corner. There were grand hopes, in both developing areas and donor-countries, for a development breakthrough based on "building on the best." Richer, better-educated, and more established entrepreneurs in LDCs were to be teamed-up with efficient financial and technological assistance from industrialized countries. The rate and amount of growth expected as a result was anticipated to be high enough to reach most if not all sectors of society, including the small-scale and/or less efficient sectors. This is the basis of the much discussed "trickle-down" effect (Rostow, 1960).

As is well-known, the trickle-down did not occur (Chenery, 1975; Adelman, 1975). The overall situation is far too complex to analyse here in any depth, but we can discuss a number of factors which, in the RD context, played a major part in the failure. A part of the strong belief in the potential for growth in agriculture had stemmed from assumptions of greater productivity based upon economies of scale that "progressive farmers" with larger holdings would be able to enjoy. Unfortunately, this did not occur, for a number of reasons. First, non-farm inputs required for large- scale production were not always available, or accessible in good time. Second, as already noted, efficient agriculture in developing countries is as much a labor-intensive as an input-intensive activity, perhaps even more so given the logistical and marketing problems faced by producers. Smaller farms, with more careful husbandry, are comparatively more efficient therefore, and the emphasis on larger producers was in that sense misplaced.

Third, existing technologies were just not good enough to achieve the production levels aspired to (this was before the arrival of the high yielding varieties), and even relatively good management in large farms was not capable of producing the quantum leaps required to meet expectations. Finally, and as we have seen in other contexts, higher profits from increased production and greater productivity do not automatically mean optimally efficient re-investment. In this case also, increases in personal consumption, financial manipulation, and speculative activities like land purchases siphoned off investable productive resources and upset calculations.

The pendulum therefore swung towards equity, and a more participatory approach to RD (Chenery's "re-distribution with growth," 1974; Streeten, 1980; Morris, 1980; Cohen and Uphoff, 1977). Instead of dramatically increasing agricultural production in limited areas it was decided to encourage comparatively limited increases in production in dramatically expanded areas. The focus of public support for human and material resources was to be broadened to include the maximum number of people. All who wanted to were to have the opportunity to actively participate in their own development. By doing this, it was hoped, a number of pitfalls of the earlier arrangements could be avoided. With attention now being paid to medium and small producers, support would go to those sectors of agricultural production which had shown themselves to be most efficient.

Further, since this support was now going to be directly provided to recipients, rather than go through the more circuitous old trickle-down route, opportunities for siphoning off the benefits would also diminish. Finally, a vast and thus far untapped human potential would be released, and the latent energies and knowledge of great masses of rural populations harnessed for development. In this way would attention to equity serve an end far greater than just itself -- it would also dramatically favor efficiency and production.

Unfortunately, these hopes were also to be substantially belied. These arrangements were put into place at about the same time that the Green Revolution came into full flower, bringing with it, as we have noted more than once so far, sharply increased asset and income disparities. Where the high yielding varieties were not used, on the other hand, equity-centered production by itself was of course still not able to show the quantum increases in product which were so sorely needed. Thus some commentators began to argue that participatory production arrangements were vastly inferior to new land-augmenting technologies, and it was the latter which needed emphasis, especially in the face of renewed threats of catastrophic famine.

The last three to four years have therefore again seen a roll-back towards the efficiency/growth pole. Its proponents argue that we are faced with terrible shortages caused by anticipated physical shortfalls in food production. Some do not believe in the participatory approach in the first place. Others do, but maintain that, while inherently beneficial, such approaches would take too long by themselves to meet the need. They should therefore be temporarily shelved, or at least heavily supplemented by large-scale production with little or no regard paid to equity considerations. Their concern is that the anticipated need for large physical quantities of food to avert worldwide famine will not be met by participatory approaches alone. Thus equity is discounted once more in favor of maximum growth.

We cannot expect to resolve these contentious issues in the confines of a few short pages. They are raised only to ensure that they assume their rightful place in the larger analyses and planning of RD. We stress here the need to think these issues through very carefully because an enormous aspect of human well-being hinges upon them. Towards that, the following assertions are offered as a starting point:

(a) adequate accumulation of capital for investment is a key element for all societies that wish to develop economically;
(b) many possible ways exist of enabling accumulation. An important issue in this context, therefore, is the question of which sections, groups, or classes in society *provide* the economic surpluses to be accumulated, who *controls* the nature, pace and direction of the investment of this surplus, and who *benefits* most from it;
(c) depending upon the route chosen, the process of accumulation has the potential to be more or less equitable. This is so for all forms of human social organization, and is not restricted to capitalist production only. The "Red vs. Expert" debates of the People's Republic of China in the late Mao era may be considered a socialist variant of this equity vs. efficiency issue, for example, as indeed would be, at a deeper level, the larger Cultural Revolution itself;
(d) the most crucial aspect of the equity *vs.* efficiency debate is the way the second term is defined. Although it presents a very precise, carefully determined, and apparently well-thought-through countenance, "efficiency," as with so many terms in social-science, is a variable concept, substantially dependent upon its underlying assumptions. And since these assumptions are not always self-evident or precise, the resulting ambiguity can lead to problems.[4]
(e) Given the above considerations, even under capitalist conditions, the provision of equity in social relations might be a lot more helpful for efficient accumulation than is commonly acknowledged.

In the forestry sector, the equity/efficiency issue often arises, though it is only rarely perceived as such. In a social forestry project, for instance, typically there is a village woodlot component and a farm forestry element, which in many ways really amount to an equity-oriented part and an efficiency-oriented part. It is usually stipulated in some fashion that the produce of the woodlot be evenly divided between village households, while the seedlings and extension advice for farm forestry are available to whoever wants them.

Characteristically, the farm forestry side is a runaway success, with farmers taking far more seedlings that were targeted and the bigger farmers making very handsome profits from their participation, while the woodlot side sags, because villagers deeply suspect a forestry department that might want to take over "their" land, find it difficult to agree on what to plant, have trouble protecting what does get planted, and all too often see most of the benefits of the woodlot going to local elites that dominate village life. In reaction to these developments, project officers understandably begin to spend more time with the farm forestry side and devote less effort and interest in the woodlot effort, just as agricultural extension agents tend to spend more time with more innnovative, sophisticated and richer farmers who take their advice than with poorer, less well educated peasants who regard them with suspicion. As Marilyn Hoskins (1982), who has a great deal of experience in Third World forestry, put it, "the model of community woodlots is not easy to apply." Promoting improved incomes for the poor, in short, is difficult both in rural development and in forestry.

---

[1] One could also argue that awareness of the protein problem probably could not have changed the policy decision in favor of foodgrain production. How could planners not urge greater foodgrain efforts once the new "Green Revolution" technology had become available, even if they had known it would mean less pulses? The first need was considered to be to provide enough calories; a balanced diet could only be secondary to that overriding goal.

[2] Interestingly, this Maharashtra Employment Guarantee Scheme furnishes a significant part of the labor input into that state's social forestry project.

[3] This assertion rests upon the observation that in Third World agriculture productivity per hectare varies inversely with size of landholding. Small farms are seen to have higher yields per unit area than big farms, principally because the former invest more labor per hectare due to their comparatively low opportunity cost of labor. Small farmers, in other words, operate higher up on the production function of a given technology than do large farmers. Documentation of these points is very

rich (see for instance, Dorner, 1972: 103ff; Owens and Shaw, 1972: 59-60 and 170; Tai, 1974: 110- 113; and Berry and Cline, 1979).

[4]The term "efficiency" as normally used in RD work is based on the following assumptions; (i) only economic variables are included in the definition; social variables are generally not included; (ii) the calculation is on a "private" as opposed to "public" basis; the two often conflict, as has been seen; (iii) some economic variables are often left out altogether in cost/benefit calculations, as for example such "externalities" as pollution costs; (iv) no distinction is made between human and non-human production inputs -- all are treated as mere commodities with no need for "special treatment" for the former; (v) perfectly competitive markets are assumed, a condition almost always honored only in its breach; (vi) based upon the historical experience of the early-industrializing nations, efficiency ratios are derived on the basis of economizing labor inputs (which in most of the Western countries have in recent history been a very expensive factor of production); obviously, this is not necessarily the case for LDCs. As an example, the much-touted superiority of US agriculture is only true on a per capita worker basis --when compared on a productivity per unit of land, energy or most other inputs, the US falls into line with other efficient producers and for certain crops is even overtaken by countries such as Japan and Egypt (Sinha, 1976)

CHAPTER 5. STRUCTURAL AND SYSTEM CONSTRAINTS

The development plans of many, perhaps even most, developing countries, tend to treat rural societies as neutral structures which are affected by, but do not influence, government RD strategy. Actually, of course, they are highly structured webs containing political, social and economic dimensions which were very firmly in place long before any RD efforts arrived on the scene. These dimensions form the human and power environments within which development projects are then introduced. Further, such environments are never neutral. Development, after all, means change, and change means that people's interests are affected. Naturally, people will try to deal with that change to their own best advantage. Those at the bottom of the rural social ladder have only labor to offer in exchange for benefits from any new RD activity. Those more fortunately positioned are able to draw on other resources (land holdings, bribe money, political influence, etc.) that are unfailingly more powerful in commanding RD benefits in the form of profits, patronage, corruption, status, and so on. This political economy of rural reality can and very often does have severe constraining effects on any RD efforts, both at local and at national levels.

A. <u>Structural Constraints at the Local Level</u>

Every rural community has a power structure of one kind or another. Exceptions to this rule do exist, as with some relatively more egalitarian hunting and gathering cultures (e.g., Turnbull, 1962 or Thomas, 1958), and possibly among various swidden societies as well, but typically rural communities are highly structured.

Ownership of productive resources and assets is generally the power base for most dominating classes, and in the Third World countryside rural power is generally vested in the ownership of land. Thus a person's (or family's or clan's) status in the village directly relates to how much land is owned or controlled. The unequal land ownership that is a characteristic of most developing countries then reflects itself in an unequal social structure.

Other resources that count in determining social position are numbers, ancestry, education, and access to non-land assets or income from within or outside the village.[1] All resources tend to be distributed unequally, and they also tend to have a cumulative effect such that each reinforces the others. As a result, those that have more land are more likely to obtain education, and so on. The overall result is a social, political and economic pyramid, with a few powerful and (at least relatively) wealthy people at the apex, and with larger groups as one moves down through the social strata to the poorest and weakest at the bottom.

It is always difficult to analyze social classes in the countryside because of the high level of human complexity that obtains in rural areas.[2] For instance, a given household might very well possess a small holding of land in several parcels scattered around the village, rent a number of these parcels to others, itself rent-in several other parcels (perhaps more adjacent to its own plots), hire out some of its labor to work for others and hire in labor in different seasonal patterns, and have some family members away in the city sending home regular remittances. Thus within one household would be farmers, landlords, sharecroppers, wage laborers and employers all at the same time.

Despite these difficulties, it is nevertheless possible to categorize households along some very rough lines. Starting with the most privileged groups, we have big farmers and/or landlords, followed by middle and small farmers. The first group produces a significant surplus every year (often enough to permit entry into money lending and other commercial/manufacturing activities), while the second derives enough on which to get by from their own land, perhaps with a modest surplus in the case of the middle farmers. Then there are the marginal farmers/sharecroppers, those who have a tenuous relationship to cultivation, and who are often in debt and hovering at the subsistence level, probably in some degree of malnutrition a good part of the time. Finally, there exists at the bottom of the social scale a group of landless or virtually landless agricultural workers.

These "poorest of the poor" always live a precarious existence, being employed at the desire and whim of the landowner, are usually heavily in debt and generally suffer chronic malnutrition. For this group, even a semi-feudal, patron-client kind of relationship with a landowner -- one which provides a modicum of security in return for lifelong immobilty and even bondage -- would be an improvement, so drastic are their conditions. Interspersed throughout the lower strata of the community are the artisan families -- carpenters, potters, barbers, etc. --who, depending on the demand for their services (which is subject both to technological displacement and to population growth -- for example, carpenters could be in trouble from either rubber-tired bullock cart wheels or too many carpenter families having too many sons), are higher or lower in the system.

Given such a social structure, it is hardly surprising that new resources coming into the village tend to follow the lines of distribution already well in place. Agricultural credit, physical inputs like fertilizer or seeds, hardware such as water pumps, and even intangibles like advice from extension agents, all seem to find their way most easily and naturally into the hands of the already large and wealthy. It should be expected, then, that rural development programs at local levels customarily follow the patterns of power and wealth already extant. Yet, what is worse, they usually reinforce and exacerbate such patterns. Thus when new forestry programs are found to benefit primarily the village rich, they are in essence following the well-worn path of most previous RD efforts.

B. Structural Constraints at the National Level

Any government has a number of key groups or structures to which it must respond, for it is the support of these entities that keeps it in power. Such support may not always be a sufficient condition for incumbency, but it is always a necessary one. If such constituencies or publics withdraw their support and/or defect, the government is almost assuredly not going to continue for very long. To ensure this support, governments generally make concerted efforts to dispense favors and patronage, with the latter commonly termed subsidies. The various constituencies in turn back the rulers and use the latter's patronage to reinforce their own position in the system.

Invariably some of these constituencies will have louder voices than others on the national level, just as was the case on the local level. Thus the military, for example, or the major banks (whether public or private), or top-level civil servants, or larger industrial concerns and important exporters and importers will all be taken very seriously indeed, while others such as social welfare organizations and public health agencies will be treated with much less concern.[3] As for such differentiation in the the rural areas, large landholders, both crop and timber related, are most often found in the former group, while sharecroppers, landless agricultural laborers and forest workers usually appear in the latter.

The influences of the more powerful constituencies serve as a powerful constraint on a government's ability and/or will to introduce change, sometimes totally immobilizing it. The term "political will" is of interest here. One often hears or reads in the development field that if only a given government had the "political will," it could work wonders -- for example introduce a real land ceiling, or set up an agricultural credit program that actually delivers loan money to small farmers and sharecroppers, or eliminate corruption. It is almost as if "political will" were deemed to be an extra ingredient that could be added as required into the development growth process: if x amount of redistribution is desired along with y rate of growth, then add z quantum of "political will" and the whole thing will work out just right.

In fact, "political will" is a direct function of the political, social and economic power structures in a country; it follows the lines of force and stress created by the distribution of power within that structure. It is for this reason that the "political will" to subsidize something like importing heavy machinery for industrial enterprises, or buying more tanks for the army is found quite easily, while the will to guarantee rights for sharecroppers or prevent siphoning off of funds in a rural public works project is so terribly hard to locate.

"Political will," in sum, is the result of very strong social pressures at all levels, overwhelmingly emanating from the privileged groups and classes, and therefore cannot be conjured up easily to oppose military hardware or to assist such groups as sharecroppers without first bringing about some change in those relationships. Not surprisingly, then, LDC governments can usually find the political will to grant timber concessions to large private interests much more easily than they are able to locate the political will to assure that a community forestry program targeted toward the rural poor actually delivers its benefits to its intended recipients.

C. Linkages Between National and Local Levels

Structural constraints on RD efforts of the types just discussed are reinforced in the rural areas by the nature of the relationships or linkages between the national and local levels (often including such intermediate tiers as state, province, and district). Those in charge at the national level need the allegiance and support of people at the local one, and the latter for their part seek patronage from the center in order to gain control of resources coming down from the central government. The result of these reinforcing needs often has been a reciprocal relationship in which local elites support national ones in return for a monopoly over the resources being funneled down to them. This arrangement puts severe constraints on many RD programs, and is often all the more difficult to deal with because it is tacit: no concrete agreements exist, no formal negotiations are held, and neither side ever openly articulates the reciprocity. Things always just seem to work out more smoothly if the central government works through the "natural" leaders of the village, if it looks for "progressive" farmers to implement its new technologies, if it does not get distracted from its goal of increasing aggregate production by getting bogged down with the petty grievances of the poor, and so on.

A major aspect of this pattern of linkages for rural development is that those involved do not easily give them up. There might be much to be said for switching resources from armaments to public health programs, and compelling arguments for such a course may very well be made on humanitarian and other grounds. However, this does not mean that a government is going to alienate its military support base in order to redistribute resources to a vaguely defined "public" that will benefit from having cleaner water or more paramedics in neighborhood dispensaries. The beneficiaries of public health initiatives may in time come to support the government, particularly if their enhanced physical well-being is augmented with education, employment, better housing and the like. But this is a long-term proposition, and a government that neglects its military constituency today in order to lay the groundwork for what may possibly be a replacement constituency at some future time is not likely still to be in power when that happy day arrives.

In much the same fashion governments are not readily going to forsake their rural landlord/big farmer public in order to redirect resources to the rural poor, in order to build up a future constituency that may someday replace the present rural elite. The risks are simply too great for remaining in power in the national capital during the interim period. Rural elites if alienated will likely cease to have the power and authority needed to maintain order and stability in the countryside. In the absence of the social control that rural elites exercise, rural insurrection becomes a real possibility, and that is something no government wishes to contemplate (Blair, 1984).

It should be pointed out and underscored that these considerations are not necessarily conscious thoughts at all levels of the linkage structure, from village up through to the national capital. For many of those involved, it is just a matter of the relative smoothness and ease of doing things in the same old ways, of continuing bureaucratic precedent, of following familiar guidelines and pathways which result in a functional support of the status quo. A government official at the local level may well find it efficient and convenient to administer a rural works project in the same way he has always done it, i.e., have local leaders select the sites, get local work chiefs to form crews and manage both the actual work and the payroll, and refer any complaints about wages or work conditions to the local constabulary, which will make sure that no one has cause to complain more than once. The same could be said about a great many forestry operations as well. That official may not be consciously supporting the status quo and obstructing change, but that is the unavoidable and unfortunate consequence of his activities nonetheless.

All this having been said, it should be noted that neither governments nor village elites are monolithic. At the national level, different agencies, and people within the same agency, often pursue different ideas and policies, while at local level different factions, groups, classes or neighborhoods often have adversarial approaches to things. This heterogeneity at the local level in many ways makes it harder to change things, for it is difficult to get agreement. However, it can also make it easier to bring about change, for what some oppose as injurious to their interest others will support as advantageous to themselves.

Nor is the fit between national and local elites a perfect one; rarely do their interests coincide completely (e.g., central governments generally want low food prices to ensure urban peace, while capitalist farmers want high food prices to maximize their own profits), and this mismatching allows change to occur. Lastly, unplanned effects of RD efforts, which are generally seen as inhibiting and blocking success, can also have favorable effects, contributing to positive rural change. The situation, in a word, is not so locked into place as our treatment of structural constraints might at first glance indicate.

D. System Constraints

Each of the resource, organization, policy, and structural constraints discussed so far is also related, at a broader level, to the overarching social system within which it operates. In this context, the term "social system" refers to the basic production relations in society -- the essential rules, regulations, and methods by and through which work and production is organized. Since social systems are all-encompassing, and contain powerful features which arbitrate most if not not all human interrelations within their domain, it is worthwhile to examine their salient characteristics in order to better understand the logic behind their historical development. Although such analyses are relevant to the whole historical range of social systems, e.g., communal, feudal, capitalist, and socialist, we restrict ourselves here to capitalist organization because that is the production system with which this paper has been most concerned. What follows is a very elementary exposition of the nature of the normal operations of capitalist production applied to our context, with particular reference to the constraints just noted.

For our purposes, we need focus on only the following elementary/basic features of capitalist production as they apply to agriculture:

(a) production is mainly for the market, if not exclusively so. Producers use the market to sell their output, as well as to buy what they themselves need. Producing for direct- or self-consumption is not the intent of the system;[4]

(b) the goal of such production is unlimited personal accumulation. No limits, other than perhaps physical or biological ones in some contexts, are set upon the individual accumulation process. Certainly there are no socially-set limits upon accumulation;

(c) taking (a) and (b) together, the object of involving oneself in the economy is to make money, not products. The latter, though important, are secondary, being produced and/or traded only to satisfy the principal requirement of financial accumulation;

(d) production is therefore undertaken on the basis of a strictly private cost- benefit calculus. The results of such a calculation may or may not lead to societal benefit. If the two converge, well and good, but if not, private considerations will prevail, even to the detriment of society;

(e) such production has an in-built tendency towards concentration/agglomeration. Expansion is a given drive in the system, at the micro- as well as the macro-levels. In its processes the weaker fall by the wayside and are either taken over or forsaken.

These "systemic" observations about production based on capitalist methods may be applied to some of the constraints discussed earlier to see how the latter are affected. First, these policy-related constraints mostly had to do with accounting for inequalities of various types (urban-rural, income, employment, regional, and efficiency). These considerations now take on a different hue. If the simple exposition given just now is correct, then inequality is a normal result of capitalist production arrangements, and as such it is highly antithetical to the equity pole of the equity/efficiency argument dealt with in Chapter 4. The task facing developmentalists is thus not a question of adjusting an essentially equitable system to keep it beneficial. Instead, and incomparably more difficult, the challenge they confront is the Herculean one of bringing some equity to a social arrangement which is inherently inequitable, and which, left to itself, has been seen to and will again degenerate into enormous inequities.

A second inference concerns the oft-discussed issue of land reform. The central importance of an equitable land-distribution and progressive land-tenure arrangements are accepted by most. A majority of observers would therefore like to see land-reform enacted in places where the distribution of land holdings is skewed. A radical redistribution of the principal asset of agricultural production is often suggested as a major step towards the elimination of rural development obstacles, if not actually as a panacea itself (for example, most recently by Prosterman and Reidigger, 1987).

Applying our analyses of systemic constraints, however, the situation seems much less sanguine. Suppose that, against all odds, a country were able to carry out a serious and genuine land reform. Some of the structural constraints in society would therefore have been removed, and all cultivators enabled to become landowners. Right from that moment, however, the tendency would once again be towards concentration of land assets if the basic social relations were not changed, i.e., if agrarian capitalism were still the system of organization and production. The *normal* workings of capitalist enterprise would once again promote inequality in social terms, and further the gradual (or not so gradual) return of a skewed land distribution.

On a less dramatic level, we might consider the issue of tree tenure, which has become a topic of considerable interest in the forestry community in recent years (e.g., Fortmann and Riddell, 1985; Raintree, 1987). If the pattern for tree ownership follows that of the ownership of the land on which they grow, as is the case for the most part in South Asia, then it will surely happen that farm forestry projects will favor those who own the land, with those owning the most land getting the most benefit, whatever equity goals the planners might have had in mind. On the other hand, in areas where statist colonial traditions endure, as in large parts of Africa, certain species, wherever they grow, are considered partially state property, in that official permission is needed to cut them (for examples, see Brechin and West, 1982; and Thomson, 1981; and Thomson et al, 1986). This in effect means that either stealth or gratuities to forestry officials are a necessary part of gaining access to these trees. Understandably, these systemic constraints have a depressing effect on local enthusiasm for growing such protected species.

In some cases, questions of tenure could be considered to hinge on much older and deeper considerations that obtain in the modern legal-administrative systems. In Cernea's (1981) account of a forestry project in Pakistan, for example, the area used for plantation had been a common waste land, but once it showed signs of becoming valuable, locally dominant elements were able to privatize it for themselves through exercising a traditional frontier settlement practice.

Third, on the administrative and organizational-behavior side, the acknowledgment of systemic constraints both helps to clarify organizational limits and suggest boundaries beyond which reform within the same social system may not be possible. For example, viewed in the context of social systems, administrative change requiring "bureaucratic reorientation" of the sort discussed in Korten and Uphoff (1981; see Chapter 7 below) becomes more complex than appears at first sight. If we assume, as we must, that bureaucrats behave the way they do because it makes eminent sense for most of them as individuals given their social reality, then reorienting them will be a comparatively more difficult, thankless, and prolonged task than is sometimes assumed.

Administrative reorientation accordingly becomes more than a matter of just addressing the shortcomings or imperfections of sensitive people in a benign way in order to make them see reason. Instead, it demands an understanding of what it is in the public servant's social framework that makes the pursuit of individual well-being require actions opposed to the interest of the people ostensibly being served, despite what might well be the administrator's own understanding of the situation and a sincere personal desire for things to be otherwise.

The point here is not whether or how capitalist agriculture leads to concentration in land, or to bureaucratized administration, etc. These examples are used only to illustrate the distinction and at the same time the interconnection between structure and system. More important is the need to note the critical place of analyses of social systems, in terms of their own inner workings, in order to see what might be expected from them through their normal operation. Indeed, one of the major challenges of such analyses is to ascertain the circumstances and extent to which resource, organizational, policy or structural constraints might be alleviated or modified while continuing to maintain the basic system, as opposed to others in which the system itself would have to undergo some change before these "second-order" effects could be countered. All in all, the importance of the normal workings of the social system in place cannot be overestimated in determining what goes on in society.

¤¤¤¤

Part II has outlined a number of constraints that constitute significant and at times daunting hurdles in the way of forestry efforts that hope to promote rural development and at the same time advance the conditions of the rural poor. In some cases these hurdles may well be impassable altogether. Social forestry is not and cannot be, as Foley and Barnard (1984: 27-28) among others point out, a panacea for rural poverty in the Third World.

But just because something is not a cure-all does not mean that it is therefore useless. These constraints are serious, to be sure, but they do not hopelessly block all progress and they do not mean that forestry enterprises are inherently incapable of making some real contribution to the rural development process and providing some amelioration to the rural poor. On the contrary, there are a number of ways to tackle these constraints that have proven effective in the rural development experience, and many of them should prove useful in forestry as well. These strategies and approaches will be the topic of Part III.

---

[1]For example, remittances sent home by temporary emigrants to the city. A new instance here is the income from foreign workers in the Middle East who send a part of their earnings home.

[2]For useful attempts at doing this, see Hinton (1968) or Crook and Crook (1979). Both studies focus on land reform in China after the communist revolution there. What is most striking about them is that even a disciplined leadership with very strong ideas about rural socio-economic class divisions found it extremely difficult and painstaking a task to decide in a single village who belonged exactly in what class. Class analysis in the abstract is fairly easily done, but in the concrete with individual households it is something else.

[3]The system described in these first two paragraphs is characteristic of the developed and developing countries alike. In the parliamentary system there is an electoral process to be taken into account, but it can be seen (in a very crude sense to be sure) as somewhat analogous to the *coup d'état*: If enough powerful constituencies are aggrieved, they generally manage to oust the incumbent officeholders in an election, just as in nonparliamentary systems they put their weight behind coups. The primary differences lie in the degree of openness of the processes of change (willingness to tolerate dissent) and in the structure of rules (for fairness, orderliness, equity, etc.) in those processes.

[4]Obviously, the many rural areas that feature considerable subsistence production are not "completely capitalist" (or one could say they exhibit "feudal remnants"), but the analysis here does apply within broad limits to those aspects of these systems that are capitalist in orientation, and it is after all precisely the capitalist elements in such systems that are so important in maintaining the status quo in terms of development.

PART III

TACKLING THE CONSTRAINTS: DEVELOPMENT INITIATIVES

In Part II we have examined at some length the many serious and even awesome hurdles standing in the way of rural development efforts. After such an analysis, particularly the consideration of structural and system constraints in Chapter 6, it may seem strange that anything positive ever happens at all in the RD field. Indeed, the whole history of RD over the last several decades is strewn with failed projects of all sorts that have run aground on one or another of the many reefs and shoals discussed in Part II.

Yet some RD projects do succeed in promoting both economic growth and improvement in the lot of the rural poor, while others have been able to deliver sustained non-economic benefits to a wide audience including the rural poor, such as a real enhancement of rural health standards or lasting adult literacy. In Part III we will look at some of the approaches, strategies and methodologies that have facilitated such successes. We begin in Chapter 6 with a consideration of *rural institutions* in the rural development process, particularly what can be called local institutions. Chapter 7 focuses on a number of rural development *strategies* that have proved successful, emphasizing particularly four that have enjoyed considerable attention in recent years: adaptive development administration; privatization; decentralization; and farming systems research. Finally, Chapter 8 will endeavor to bring in some answers to the questions about *equity and balance* in rural development that we raised at several points in Part II.

CHAPTER 6. RURAL INSTITUTIONS AND DEVELOPMENT

By custom in the social sciences, an institution is defined as any human activity that is repeated systematically over time. It follows, then, that all rural development strategies adopted by governments must necessarily be fashioned in one way or another, around rural institutions (RIs). This chapter briefly examines the kinds of RIs that are involved in RD, and then focuses upon one particular form of RI considered especially effective for promoting RD -- that of local organization (LO). Among their many other attributes, LOs show considerable promise in being able to counter many of the constraints discussed in the previous chapter. Their potential for contribution to the forestry sector also appears high, and they could very well play a key role in development forestry.

A. The Universe of Rural Institutions and the Central Importance of Local Organizations

RIs are perhaps best thought of as *channels* through which rural people govern local activities, organize themselves both for economic endeavor and to obtain public goods, and articulate their problems and needs to "higher level" political and administrative systems. Even where no clearly defined "community" exists around which to organize for such purposes, people or groups of people can often find a number of alternative channels through which to structure their involvement in RD activities.

These channels have been identified by previous studies[1] of rural institutions and participation in rural development. They represent seven major categories of communication and cooperation between rural people and their economic and administrative environment, arranged along a rough public-to-private dimension:

A. central/federal government agencies
B. parastatal bodies
C. local government
D. local organizations
E. political associations
F. local (small scale) private enterprise
G. large-scale private enterprise

We should note that these categories have been established to serve as an analytical aid towards a better understanding of RIs. As such, they are in no way sacrosanct, or unchangable. They have been useful in a general context, but there are sure to exist particular situations which would demand amendments and alterations in their structure and logic. As it is, we may note even now the potential for adjustment because of the existence of overlaps between certain of these categorizations. For example, some production co-operatives, though formally public sector organizations, might very well be engaged in activities which are hard to distinguish from those of private enterprises. Or parastatal organizations (such as forestry development corporations) might also resemble private enterprise in their trading and production functions. Thus it would be advisable to use this categorization discerningly and with caution, duly adjusting it to suit specific circumstances.

One of these seven major channels is local organization. In an array like the one presented here, it falls just about at the center. In fact, LOs have something of a unique quality in that they often manage to blend in one body the best qualities of the public and private sectors -- the accountability of the former with the incentive-providing capability of the latter. This very valuable intermediate ground is not held by any of the other six.

There are two other dimensions along which LOs stand out from other rural institutions. One distinguishing feature relates to their accountability to participating members. LOs are directly accountable to their memberships, while other RIs, moving off towards both the public (governmental) and private directions, are not membership organizations. The other characteristic is that LOs are primarily involved in locally-oriented activities -- an attribute that may or may not apply in the case of other RIs.[2]

These three dimensions -- whether RIs are (1) public or private, (2) membership or non-membership based, and (3) locally or externally oriented/directed -- may be used to illustrate graphically the relationship of the various types of RIs to each other, as is done in Figure 1,[3] which also gives a "score" for each type of RI along each dimension.

Figure 1

RURAL INSTITUTIONS LOCATED ALONG THREE DIMENSIONS

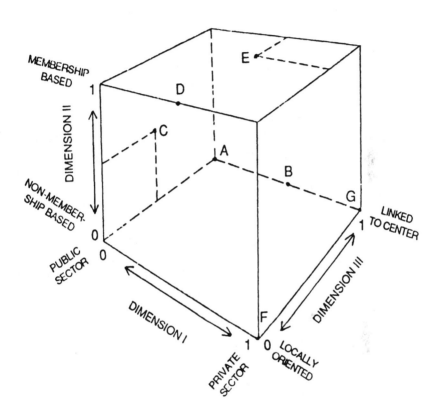

TYPE OF INSTITUTION	DIMENSION AND SCORE		
	I	II	III
A. Central/federal government agencies	0	0	1
B. Parastatal bodies	0.5	0	1
C. Local governments	0	0.5	0.5
D. Local organizations	0.5	1	0
E. Political associations	0.5	1	0.75
F. Local private enterprises	1	0	0
G. Large-scale private enterprises	1	0	1

A. *Central/federal government agencies* are fully in the public sector, so they score a "0" on Dimension I. They are non-membership based (score = 0 on Dimension II also), and *not* locally oriented (score = 1 on Dimension III).

B. *Parastatal bodies* (e.g., tea marketing boards, commodity export corporations, etc.) are normally held or owned fully by the government/public sector, but operate to a greater or lesser extent as does the private sector, and in competition either with it or perhaps with other parastatals, such as tea boards in different countries competing for the world market. Forestry development corporations are similar. They thus rank between the public and private sectors on Dimension I (score = 0.5). On the second and third dimensions, though, they receive the same rating as the "pure" government agencies (score = 0 and 1 respectively).

C. *Local governments*, although totally in the public-sector (Dimension I score = 0) often do retain, at least partly, a membership base through appointments or elections (score = 0.5 on II). Also, by reason of their function as channelers of support upwards and patronage downwards, they are linked to both village (local) and center (non-local), and so draw another 0.5 rating for Dimension III.

Let us skip item D, *Local Organizations*, for the moment and return to it last.

E. *Political associations* are usually completely membership based (II = 1), centrally oriented, albeit with some local base (III = 0.75) and really neither public nor private (I = 0.5).

F&G. *Private enterprise* is clearly at the high end of Dimension I (score = 1) and low end of Dimension II (score = 0). Within this category, local level (and small scale) enterprises (F) are locally oriented (III = 0), while large scale enterprises (G) are more centrally focused (III = 1).

This brings us to the last remaining category of the range of RIs, the local organizations; we distinguish LOs from the others in that they are:

(a) *both public and private*, inasmuch as they are part of the common domain, and thus subject to public accountability, yet also usually concerned with producing, processing, or distributing some good or service that is essentially private (I = 0.5);

(b) *membership based* bodies, as opposed to governmental organizations or private enterprise, neither of which normally have members, except in the sense of career recruitment, as with a forestry department "cadre" (II = 1);

(c) *locally oriented*, rather than linked to external connections/centers either through administrative control (as with governmental agencies or political associations) or through market/economic ties (as with private businesses) (III = 0).

This particular blend of (a) public accountability with private-style incentive generation, (b) membership-based recruitment, mobilization, and training, and (c) a local orientation, is what makes LOs the potentially powerful engines of RD that they are.

The LO designation includes many institutions of the type often called non-government organizations (NGOs) or private voluntary organizations. There are, however, several problems in drawing exact parallels between the terms. For one thing, some NGOs are much larger than local, and so would not be included (though if sufficiently autonomous, local units of an NGO would be *de facto* LOs). Second, the term NGO itself lends a certain degree of confusion here, for it implies that an organization is in the private sector, that is, that it is *not* governmental. True enough, but when one then begins to consider how the private sector is usually defined, the picture begins to become a bit murky, for one of the principal characteristics of the "private sector" is that making a profit from the marketplace is at the top of its priorities. Making a profit *may* be a goal of any given LO (e.g., a group savings and credit organization), but not necessarily (e.g., a local women's club focusing primarily on child health and nutrition). Thus while some NGOs are LOs and some LOs are NGOs, the overlap is by no means complete; some institutions can be either without also being the other. For this reason, we have used the term NGO relatively infrequently.

B. Types of Local Organizations

In keeping with the broader group of rural institutions of which they are a part, local organizations are difficult to classify into analytical categories. They are both too numerous and too complex to be definitively differentiated. They can be organized along any number of lines both internally and in their relationships with other bodies and institutions as well, plus they have had such wide local variations across history and culture that any generalizations would be hazardous.

Yet LOs constitute an interesting and even crucial area of analysis and understanding in the overall context of rural development, one which demands attention in spite of its conceptual problems and potential pitfalls. The Rural Development Committee at Cornell University has been involved in just such an effort over the last decade or so, under the leadership of Milton Esman and Norman Uphoff. What follows is a brief précis of the current state of thinking regarding local organizations, based largely upon their most recent published work (Esman & Uphoff, 1984, Chapter 3). These authors first identify five salient features of local organizations, and then use these characteristics to distinguish three major LO categories. We will review each in turn.

i. Principal characteristics of LOs

Esman and Uphoff reason their way through a mass of the essential and practical detail associated with LOs,[4] and then settle upon five features as representing the analytical essence of that form of rural institution. They are: the membership base, the source of authority and of legitimacy, the rationale behind or purpose of the body, the nature and extent of functions performed, and the origin of the resource support.

> (a) *Membership*. This feature deals with the LO's membership base, looking to its nature and origins. Considerations of how similar or diverse the membership, the extent of its homo-/heterogeneity, reasons for members associating with each other and the nature of the bonds between them all come under this purview.

> (b) *Authority*. What is the basis of the LO's legitimacy? Where does its authority come from? Is authority externally determined, from outside the LO, or is it voluntarily reciprocal within the membership? If the former, is the authorizing factor governmental

or private? These are the types of issues considered under this characteristic of LOs.

(c) *Rationale/purpose*. Obviously the reasons behind why various types of LOs are formed, and their differing purposes, represent an essential element of their nature. This is especially so given the almost infinite variation in the organizations themselves, which stretch from those associated with fully public goods to totally private ones, from manufacture and production to consumption, and from the provision of a complete line of goods and services to offering limited specialties.

(d) *Functions*. The purposes for which LOs are formed naturally have a lot to do with the functions undertaken subsequently. Here a key question is about the number of functions an LO attempts. Research has shown that, for different types of rationales and goals, varying levels of functions are necessary in an LO. Some ends are best served by single-function organizations, others by comprehensive or multiple-function efforts.

(e) *Resource base*. Finally, where do the LO's resources come from? Are they voluntarily contributed or levied in some way? Are they, in addition or instead, externally raised? From what source(s)? Are those sources public or private? The financial and other resource underpinnings of LOs are crucial in any analysis attempted of them, and represent the fifth and final important characteristic in the Esman/Uphoff schema.

ii. Typology of LOs

Using the five main characteristics enumerated above, Esman and Uphoff identify three broad sub-categories of LOs: local development associations, cooperatives, and interest associations (Figure 2). Once again, although the differentiating characteristics as applied here are fairly categorical, the actual differences between the three types of LOs may not be as clear cut, especially as regards their constituencies and functions. However, with the judicious use of this framework, a number of useful insights can be achieved and the groundwork laid for further sophistication. The three LO sub-divisions are distinguished from each other by the unique application, in each case, of one of the LO characteristics.

Figure 2

TYPES OF LOCAL ORGANIZATIONS (LOs)

Characteristics of LOs	Local Development Associations (LDAs)	Cooperatives	Interest Associations
Nature of *membership* & operating *principle(s)*	decided by place of residence (heterogeneity depends on area covered)	contribution of economic resources (land, labor, capital), sharing of returns	personal characteristics and common interests
Authority and legitimization	quasi-authoritative, may have governmental	democratic decision making, may be registered and regulated	*de facto* only, conceded by members
Rationale and purpose	improve quality of life and opportunity for area residents	increase benefits from economic production and consumption	advance common interest
Function(s)	multiple functions, on area basis	single or multi-purpose, mainly in private goods and services	single or multi-purpose
Resources: base and origins	contributions, assessments or taxes, government subsidy	members' resources, government subsidy	fees and duties

(a) *Local development associations* (LDAs) are clearly differentiable using the *function* characteristic. Of the three, they alone are always multi-functional, and are (by definition) formed on a geographical basis. Cooperatives and interest associations may or may not be multi-functional, plus they are rarely (if ever) organized on the basis of area alone.

(b) *Cooperatives* have, as their distinguishing characteristic, the way they raise their *resources*. They raise their resources primarily from their own memberships (though not always soley in this way by any means, for often coops receive substantial government subsidies). Again, this feature may obtain from time to time in the other forms of LOs too, but in the case of cooperatives it is ubiquitous to the extent of becoming a defining characteristic.

(c) Finally, *interest associations* are linked to the *membership* characteristic as their distinguishing feature. As with the other two types of LOs, they may be single or multifunctional, and they may raise resources internally or externally, but neither of these qualities is important or consistent enough to define them. Instead, the interest association stands out by virtue of the composition of its members. Members of interest associations invariably either perform or relate to common tasks, or have other common features much as sex, occupation or status, an attribute not similarly mandatory for the other two.

Other differences also exist of course between the three (e.g., cooperatives normally accrue benefits to members in "private" ways as opposed to "public" ones for LDAs, and most interest associations are less broad-based than LDAs but wider than cooperatives), but these are secondary separations, neither essential nor consistent enough to be prime differentiators.

iii. Tasks of Local Organizations (by Peter May[5])

Four broad task areas may be identified for local organizations, each further subdivided into two functional categories (Figure 3). They cover the gamut of LO activity from internal organization (a) through to relations with the external environment (d), with the inputs and outputs of organizations -- resources and services respectively, falling in between.

Figure 3

TASK AREAS OF RURAL INSTITUTIONS

(a) **Intra-Organizational Tasks**
   (i) Planning and Goal-Setting
   (ii) Conflict Management

(b) **Resource Tasks**
   (i) Resource Mobilization
   (ii) Resource Management

(c) **Service Tasks**
   (i) Service provision
   (ii) Service integration

(d) **Extra-Organizational**
   (i) Control of Bureaucracy
   (ii) Claim-making on government

(a) *Intra-organizational tasks.* The *planning and goal-setting* tasks of LOs are important contributors to overall performance. The extent to which knowledge of local problems, and consensus concerning ways of resolving them, evolves through the process of project planning has an important bearing on ultimate success. This is true no matter what type of organization is involved. Locally-initiated, consultative, and/or shared approaches to gathering information and identifying what can be done within local constraints and opportunities can be decisive in ensuring that goals and objectives are set realistically.

In this connection, the "learning process" approach suggested by Korten (1980) and others should have widespread applicability. This approach focuses on participation-induced change in the implementation phase of projects, and is taken up in detail in Chapter 7. However, participation is critical for the planning phase also.[6] Just as success is often elusive when project implementation is carried out strictly and only according to blueprints imposed from a higher level, so is it also that matters take a turn for the worse when planning and goal-setting are not conducted in a participatory environment.

Conflict management is another internal task which is important, particularly where sensitive issues of land allocation and/or distribution of rewards from resource management are at stake. Up to a certain point, it is useful to view conflict itself as not totally undesirable, but rather as a positive indicator of involvement and concern on the part of rural people regarding the performance of the institutions that serve them, a sign that an enterprise is important enough for people to express views about their stakes in it. The important thing, accordingly, is not to suppress conflict (which implies a dominance of one interest over all the rest), but rather to resolve it in such a way that all who do have such a stake are included. The ability of an organization to manage and channel conflict between members in productive ways is a function of leadership, and the strength of egalitarian or participatory norms inculcated in the membership.

An example would be the ability of a local government institution to manage conflict between one village faction (say, one that wished to use a village woodlot for poles) and another (that wanted the woodlot for fodder). Conflict management is also needed at higher levels, where departmental officials need to mediate between organizational units and institutions that disagree. For example, various government agencies responsible for supplying different agricultural inputs might vie for limited foreign exchange for imports, or for other financial resources. Such competitive conflict is of course a good sign that officials are active and serious about their responsibilities, but it obviously has to be kept within reasonable bounds.

If not creatively managed, conflict can of course become detrimental and even fatal to rural institutions. The extent to which these more serious problems may be anticipated and countered varies with the type of organization. Heterogeneous and multi-purpose organizations involving entire residential settlements are more apt to experience debilitating conflict among members representing different ethnic or racial divisions, and among members controlling different amounts or quality of assets. For this reason, it may be appropriate, in programming development activities including those related to forests, to focus on smaller units than, say, entire villages. Anderson's observation on the Philippine *barangay* could be made of countless other cultures around the world:

> There exists only a limited sense of group identity and of strong obligation to the *barangay* as a whole. ... It is very weakly organized to solve *barangay*-wide internal problems or to protect residents against outside forces.... [But] on a narrower than community-wide basis, persons organized with reference to husbanding a common resource, religious organizations, irrigation communals, youth clubs and so on can demand committed participation from individuals who join in them (Anderson, 1982: 253).

In many cases, then, it may be desirable to focus organizationally on small homogeneous units, so as to reduce conflict among members and to ensure that the kind of normal social pressure applied by members of small groups can play a positive role. In other situations, of course, conflict may sometimes be helpful in motivating collective action, and larger group size could enhance the scope of participation as well as the securing of external resources. The advantages of smaller organizations, in other words, are not unqualified.

(b) *Resource tasks.* These require a subtle balance between external support, and internal reliance and accountability to participants, to secure adequate and sustainable results. *Resource mobilization,* both at the outset and throughout the execution of project activity, is affected by the quality of leadership and the extent to which members develop a sense of proprietorship over the results of their efforts. If the primary investment of financial, physical and human resources originates outside the group expected to benefit from them, a pattern of dependency may be inculcated from which it is difficult to break away without weakening institutional performance. Impetus for the continued maintenance of existing facilities and services, and diversification into new ones will then always require an external initiative. Clearly many examples of this phenomena exist; a particularly illustrative one is to be found in Blustain's study (1982), which carefully documents, in the context of the Development Committees in Jamaica, how such a dependent relationship came about which kept farmers locked in "clientelism," and prevented self-reliant progress on their part.

Conditions favoring or inhibiting resource mobilization may also be expected to differ between types of institutions and functions. The willingness of rural people to invest resources is highly dependent upon the existence of a shared awareness of the problem to be tackled, as well as upon confidence in the expectations of benefiting from the results of their investment. Activities which appear too risky -- either in terms of possible total failure or of returns not commensurate with the uncertainty involved -- or which do not seem to meet felt needs, will not prove popular.

Managing resources once mobilized so as to progress from intent to achievement is a task area which demands skill and honesty of those who are placed in control of the resources, or who became responsible for coordinating their management. Since for all practical purposes most resources, both of the physical as well as the financial type, are very scarce, the importance of their proper management cannot be gainsaid. This is where the existence and/or provision of appropriate technical skills becomes imperative. It is also one area where outside institutions can play a helpful role, through the provision of training, the inculcation of protective attitudes towards the resources, the conducting of periodic research to assess progress and constraints, and the suggestion of possible avenues for improvement in management practices. Of course the outside agency should also take advantage of the opportunity to learn from local people, who are likely to know best the qualities and limitations of the physical resources they have at their disposal. Thus another opportunity arises for a learning process on both sides.

Motivating honest management of finances or stocks of goods is potentially more difficult, and must rely in the first instance on the careful selection of managers. Here again, local members may be the best judges. A process of self-selection of leaders best suited to the demands of new enterprises may also be beneficial. In following the progress of "institutional organizers" for irrigation management in Sri Lanka, Uphoff (1987) has noted that those who emerged as good leaders were not necessarily those who already held local offices or had links with outside patrons. Rather, they were people who, through the process of project development and execution, showed their talents and earned local respect as motivators and transmitters of technical understanding. A similar approach for stimulating new leadership might well bear fruitful results in overall forestry development.

(c) *Service tasks*. The *provision and integration of services* is the essence of most rural institutions -- if they do not perform well on that score, there is little incentive for local people to continue to support them, unless, of course, as with government agencies, such backing is mandated through national or other law, and coerced support is scarcely a reliable reed to lean on, as Scott (1985) shows so well in his study of everyday peasant resistance to authority in rural Malaysia. Rural institutions may provide services either autonomously or in collaboration with external institutional support. Unfortunately, the potential gains derived from using LOs as service providers have so far not been widely appreciated, although these benefits can include mobilization of local resources and participation in service distribution to assure broad benefit.

(d) *Extra-organizational tasks*. Finally, adequate coordination of services in the local interest implies some degree of *control over the bureaucracy* and on some ability at *claim-making* by rural institutions. These tasks of LOs help to avert abuses of authority and avoid the fragmentation of resources as they are channelled through government agencies to the local level. Individuals who are eligible for services or funds are generally aware of failures to deliver on the part of the bureaucracy, but usually they can only make claims through collective channels of the sort that LOs can be very effective at providing. LOs are not the only mechanism for excercising control and claim-making, we should note. Local control can also be exercised through participation of rural institutions other than LOs (village governments, for instance, or local cells of national political parties) in the planning of government activity, and through the political process in representative government (that is, when elected officials actually are responsive and accountable to their electorates).

C. The Role of Participation

The value of people's direct participation in RD has only been recognized and acknowledged fairly recently. Previously, the idea of broad masses of people having an important -- let alone crucial -- say in the matter of their own development was comparatively rare. So was the notion that the common person had the potential wherewithal to take charge of his or her own destiny. Instead, as we have noted, most development efforts relied on the relatively few but more privileged elements in society to provide the main impetus. These were the already advantaged -- people currently in control through their ownership of productive assets, including technical knowledge and managerial skill and competence. It was reasoned that concentrating on them would provide a head start in the development race, since the least amount of time and effort would be needed to get things going. Once development occurred, all would benefit, including the broader masses, from the jobs and incomes which would be produced.

Two observations can be made about this brief description of earlier development efforts. First, that people's participation in them was almost non-existent, and even where it was present it was essentially restricted to involvement with some of the benefits of development. Second, the model substantially failed to achieve the type and level of development sought. A number of prominent scholars and practitioners linked these two aspects and concluded, among other things, that participation at the broadest possible levels was one of the most important keys to development, if not actually the most critical one (Cohen and Uphoff, 1977; Goulet, 1971; Grant, 1973). So important was it, in fact, that it could and should even be considered a goal in itself, in addition to being an important means towards other related goals (Seers, 1969). Thus participation should be placed near the top of the development agenda, and at the very least its purview should be extended beyond participation merely in benefits to include involvement in decision-making regarding planning, implementation, and evaluation.

The overriding importance of participation has gradually come to be accepted in the intervening years. Despite the many remaining problems about how best to define and appropriately measure the concept, both theoretical and empirical works have exhibited a growing competence and sophistication in studying the idea. In the area of participation in decision-making especially, particularly regarding its positive effects on project performance, there has been significant work, much of it substantiating earlier theoretical assertions (see, e.g., Fortmann and Roe, 1981; Goldsmith and Blustain, 1980; Kneerim, 1980; Wasserstrom, 1982; Morss et. al., 1976; World Bank, 1976).

Since participation does not take place in a vacuum, its socio-economic framework has a major bearing on its nature, extent and effectiveness. A multitude of social processes and institutions are reckoned to affect the participatory process, and LOs are acknowledged in this context to be some of the most powerful and progressive forces for the latter.

LOs share a reciprocal and mutually beneficial relationship with participation, helping to foster participation in a number of ways. One of their key purposes is to provide a grassroots-created and -based intermediary body between government/public agencies and individual people. As we have seen, this can help in both receiving and equitably disbursing resources and revenues from government, as well as in making demands and claims upon the latter. On the receipt-and-disbursement side, governments are increasingly coming to realize that they do not have adequate resources to provide the desired level of services to individual households. Their capabilities, even where comparatively strong, are normally sufficient only to deal with larger groups of rural populations, groups which are often several levels more aggregated than basic households.

Naturally, such valuable attributes as sensitivity, responsiveness and attention to detail suffer as a result. LOs are equipped to effectively counter this shortcoming. If genuinely motivated and participatory, they can usefully serve to organize individual households into groups to maximum benefit and effect. Especially in the all-important area of the proper disbursement of public resources, LOs can foster participatory, and therefore equitable, sharing of benefits. Similarly, on the demand and/or claim making side, LOs are instrumental in ensuring the participation of local level people and administration by helping to serve as an organized voice of the people. In both capacities, therefore, LOs enable grassroots participation, because it is only through them that the fragmented strength of comparatively powerless individual people and households is gathered and aggregated into a combined and purposeful total for RD.

Just as LOs can enhance participation, so too participation can come to the aid of LOs. The latter are prone to a frighteningly large number of "vulnerabilities", as Esman and Uphoff (1984: 181-202) term them, including resistance from the outside, internal dissensions and fissures, ineffectiveness of action, malpractices (including corruption), and subordination to external factors, including (and especially) to government. The introduction or increase of participation can be shown to be an always necessary, and sometimes even individually sufficient, factor in the control or elimination of these problems. Greater, and joint, involvement by the people in such matters as contributing (additional) resources, sharing responsibilities, resolving divisions, and holding leaderships accountable goes a long way towards improving the health and functioning ability of LOs. Perhaps nowhere is this so clear as in the context of defending LOs against the marauding influence of would-be subordinators, particularly governmental bodies.

Even though many public-sector functionaries realize the place and importance of LOs in helping governments deal with RD problems in a truly effective way, governmental interference with and subordination of these institutions is always a factor to be reckoned with. This can happen for a number of reasons, only one of which is intent (when governments decide, most likely out of the fear of losing control, that they have to "take the LOs in hand"). Even where government agencies are supportive of LOs, subordination can still take place, sometimes even from motivations of paternalism and good intentions (e.g., Thai Khadi Research Institute, 1980, or Haragopal, 1980: 45). Government interference also arises out of the "normal" leverage and control all givers of assistance gain over their beneficiaries as a matter of course. Or local elites can use their influence with higher level governmental authorities to try to take over LOs. In all these cases, participation can be a good antidote.

D. Rural Institutions, Local Organizations, Participation and Forestry

At first blush, it might appear that local organizations had little relevance to the forestry sector, inasmuch as forestry projects are typically undertaken in the public sector and so would fit into the governmental agency (A) category of Figure 1 or, in the case of forestry development corporations, possibly the parastatal (B) category. Both these types are a considerable distance from the local organization (D) type along all three dimensions of Figure 1.

Yet some of the outstanding success stories in social forestry have been achieved by just such local organizations as we have been discussing in Chapter 6. An excellent example here is the "Chipko Movement" of the Garhwal Hills in the Himalayan area of India, which is by now familiar to many people in the forestry field (see, for example, Bahuguna, 1986; Jain, 1984; Shiva and Bandyopadhyay, 1986; and more generally, Guha, 1985). Here timber cutters working in connivance with forestry officials were in the midst of a large-scale assault on the source of livelihood for a local wood products cooperative that had just been set up. Local women fastened themselves to the trees to protect them as local leadership was able to generate widespread publicity for the movement. In fairly short order outside sympathy and support built up to the point where the government found itself having to declare a moritorium on tree cutting by concessionaires.

An even better known forestry LO has been the Village Forestry Associations (VFAs) of South Korea (Eckholm, 1979; FAO, 1980; Gregersen, 1982). The VFAs are in a sense local governmental units in that they were set up by the state in the 1970s and have a governmental mandate to plant and care for local forests on both public and private land, a mandate which included army backing against recalcitrant landowners. But at the same time the VFAs are membership-based, with household heads in a village as the participants. They elect their own officers, and they produce and market a wide variety of forest-based goods such as fiber wallpaper and oak mushrooms (the aggregate value of their export products was almost $US 125 million by 1978; Gregersen, 1982: 55-56). Perhaps most important from our perspective, the two million members that belonged to more than 20,000 VFAs "perceive [the VFAs] as being institutions run by villagers themselves," in the words of one knowledgable observer (Gregersen, 1982: 41). Thus they are a combination of public and private sector aspects, they are locally oriented (though with strong ties upwards), and they are membership-based.

The VFAs are also the product of many years and decades of concern with problems of deforestation and fuelwood shortage, soil erosion and consequent agricultural production losses, and steadily growing industrial timber requirements. Various plans and structures had been developed over the years to deal with these problems, but to little effect. Still, the experience was invaluable in helping put together the 10-year plan that was launched in 1973 as an aspect of the *Saemaul Undong* (New Community Movement). In the new effort the government made a very substantial commitment to its forest development plan in terms of staffing, training, extension and forestry research. Needless to say, all this cost a great deal of money; Gregersen (1982: 45-46) cites one estimate of $US 180 million for government funding during the plan (while villagers were to contribute an additional $US 160 million, mainly in kind). Arnold's (1983: 188) estimate is even higher, at $US 600 million altogether from all sources. The VFA success, in sum, had a long history and did not come cheaply, but it was unquestionably a major achievement in social forestry and warrants attention as a model.

Particpation in forestry enterprises of course need not be confined to the local organization category. It is eminently feasible and practical in any of the other six types of rural institutions shown in Figure 1. We have seen earlier that incorporation of "rural people's knowledge" necessitates a great deal of popular participation in all project phases. Aside from their knowledge, rural people must contribute their time, energy and enthusiasm to some degree if projects are to succeed. Lack of such participation in planning and implementation has spelt the doom of a good many forestry projects that would fit into type A in Figure 1 (central/federal government agencies), as for instance Bonkoungou and Catinot (1986) report for the Sahelian region. Arnold (1987: 125) offers a similar story from Malawi. In contrast, Heermans (1985/6) finds a government-managed social forestry project in Niger to have been quite successful, largely because of its conscientious focus on particpation. Local governments (type C in Figure 1) offer more examples, for instance in panchayat (village government) managed community woodlots in India that would have been more successful if villagers had participated in project design. For if their views had been taken into account, they would undoubtedly have given construction timber and fodder a higher priority than fuelwood (Blair, 1986a). In Nepal, after an unhappy experience in attempting to manage forest lands centrally, the government has begun to turn village forest lands over to local government with considerable success (Arnold and Campbell, 1986; see also Hoskins, 1983). Participation is a crucial aspect indeed for

RD, and we shall return to it later on in Chapter 7, under the rubric of adaptive development administration.

---

[1] Much of the discussion here follows the path charted out in earlier Rural Development Committee studies from Cornell University. See in particular Uphoff, Cohen and Goldsmith (1979), and Esman and Uphoff (1982 and 1984).

[2] The term "local" is a vague one, but by it we mean a level "higher" than the household, yet "lower" than the regional level, i.e., lower than province, district or county levels, and in addition lower than subdistricts, blocks, townships, or the like. Most generally, "local" would refer to village level, but it could also mean neighborhood, community, or the like. See Uphoff (1986b: 10-14) for an attempt to pin down this elusive term.

[3] For a somewhat similar scheme, though one differing in detail, see Esman and Uphoff (1982: 21ff.).

[4] Uphoff (1986b) has recently published details for more than eighty of the case studies taken up in the Cornell RDC's LO project; the larger Esman and Uphoff (1984) work collects and analyses some 150 LO case studes in the aggregate.

[5] This section was written largely by Peter May for a shorter and earlier version of the present study.

[6] As in most of the development literature, we conceive of the "project cycle" to consist of several phases, which can be conveniently labeled planning (or planning and design), implementation, benefits (or outputs, results, etc.) and evaluation.

CHAPTER 7. RURAL DEVELOPMENT STRATEGIES

In the previous chapter we looked at the central role and function of rural institutions as vehicles for promoting development. But having an appropriate mechanism gives little help in determining direction: where is the vehicle going to go? Now it is time to take up strategies to provide that direction for rural institutions. The chapter begins with some attention to the range of change that is possible in rural development, and then proceeds to lay out a brief exposition of several of the strategies for change that have lately been in favor among both donor institutions and Third World governments for promoting rural development.

A. The Spectrum of Institutional Change

Every institution is always in a state of *some* change, even if strenuous efforts are expended to prevent any change from occurring. For example, key personnel leave the organization and are replaced, managers get rotated to new positions and begin to do things differently, etc. On the financial side, budgets expand and contract, encouraging growth and hiring, or requiring contraction and firing. The external environment also changes continually as new constituencies arise, old ones decline, and social institutions and structures keep on adjusting. Change is a generic part of the human condition, and present therefore even in efforts to delay or forestall it.

Institutions sometimes go through the motions of change, but without meaning to actually effect it. New governments or ministries, for example, may issue directives demanding sweeping changes, but institutions within the governmental structure hope to avoid implementing the new marching orders. They pay lip-service to whatever needs to be done in order to create a façade of improvement, while all the time dragging their feet in reality. Even here, change does take place, although of course it is of a nature and extent which is far short of that intended from higher level. Nevertheless, some adjustments and variations do result even from mere lip-service -- changes which, although marginal, are still greater than intended by the foot-dragging institution itself.

On the other hand, though, virutally never is there a complete change in institutions. Even after major revolutions, many -- in fact most -- of the basic functions in society must still be discharged and really cannot be changed significantly. Public order needs to be maintained, health emergencies dealt with, education provided, food produced and distributed, and so on. In addition, any post-revolutionary "new order" has perforce to depend upon the same people who provided all the services in the old one, certainly during the initial period after the takeover. So it is, then, that in the United States after 1776, in France after 1789, in Russia after 1917 and in China after 1949, all these necessary activities continued, and for the most part, except at the highest decision making levels, they continued to be carried out by the same people doing the same things in much the same way.

Most change, however, actually takes place somewhere between these two end points in the continuum as shown in Figure 4. The schema might be best explained using agricultural credit agencies as an example. The first category represents attempts to maintain the *status quo*, a policy which, as just pointed out, can never completely be effective. Next comes *upgrading*, which involves a conscious effort to improve the skills and capacities of individuals within the institution, typically through in-house short courses or external schooling. This type of change is often referred to as "professional development." The third level is *restaffing*, or replacement of individuals within the organization. An example might be the dismissal of all district-level extension officers in an agricultural ministry who had not completed bachelor's level training by a specified date and their replacement by others who had done so. Another example would be the firing of all loan agents who had not met their targets for loan issue within a calendar year.

The fourth level of institutional change is *improvement*, by which is meant developing and implementing better procedures within the organization.[1] Here a credit agency might decide to adopt a "Training and Visit" (T & V) approach in which some agents would specialize in animal husbandry, others in foodgrain crops, and so on. Next comes *reform*, or the replacement of one procedure by another, and/or the taking on of altogether new functions. An illustration here would be the replacement of an agricultural credit system, that had used loan agents based in a district headquarters and radiating out to the countryside, with a new approach in which credit-giving units were set up at lower levels (say, one for every twenty villages) and farmers would come to them for loans.

Figure 4

THE SPECTRUM OF INSTITUTIONAL CHANGE

TYPE OF CHANGE	STATUS QUO	UPGRADING	RESTAFFING	IMPROVEMENT	REFORM	RESTRUCTURING	REVOLUTION
	1	2	3	4	5	6	7
DESCRIPTION OF CHANGE	As little change as possible (but some nonetheless)	Individual improvement and professional development	Individual replacement	Procedural improvement	Procedural replacement	Institutional replacement	System replacement (but still much continuity)

Restructuring represents the sixth level of change, in which the institution itself is scrapped in order to be replaced with another. For example, the whole rural credit setup might be eliminated and a new cooperative federation placed in its stead. Finally, there is *revolution*, in which the entire system, including its local structures, national alignments, and the linkages between them, is all thrown out and replaced with a new one. Revolution is by definition intense change, but as we have seen, continuity does remain here also. For instance, some form of agricultural credit and extension will still be needed, albeit perhaps on a collective basis, and chances are that many of the old functionaries would still be around administering the new programs.

This typology of institutional change is of course only an abstract one, and concrete cases will not always easily fit exactly into one category or another. However, two points do remain: one, that there is a spectrum of change and, secondly, that change of one sort or another is always going on, planned and/or unplanned, even in situations of seeming constancy. Especially at their senior levels, institutions are constantly trying to change one thing or another. Armies plan new strategies and tactics, corporations find their old approaches inadequate and look for new ones, administrative agencies come under pressure to expand or modify their missions, and all strive to ensure their own institutional health, security, and reproduction/continuance. Such changes are far from easy to carry through though. Generals want to refight the last war, corporate managers desire to retain methods that built the company in the past, and public officials also would like to avoid painful adjustment.

Most of the changes we will be dealing with in the remainder of this chapter focus on the fourth and fifth types shown in Figure 4 -- procedural improvement and replacement. The other types are certainly possible avenues for improving RD efforts, and all of them have been employed at one time or another, but the changes that appear to have had the most effect have tended to be those clustering in the center-right area of Figure 4, so we will restrict our analysis to them.

B. Adaptive Development Adminstration

A number of the innovations in rural development administration that have been suggested in recent years reflect an urge to introduce change at various points along the spectrum discussed in the previous section. These suggestions have been given a variety of labels, such as "learning process approach" (Korten, 1980), "bureaucratic reorientation" (Korten and Uphoff, 1981), "adjunctive and strategic planning" (Rondinelli, 1983), "new professionalism" and "reversals" (both Chambers, 1983), and "social learning" (White, 1987), all of which we have tried to subsume under our phrase "adaptive development administration," or ADA. Many of these ADA concepts have found official sanction in the international donor community (e.g., World Bank, 1983: ch. 9-11).

The basic idea underlying most suggestions for ADA is a straightforward one: more bottom-up participation at all phases of the project cycle, both within the development bureaucracy itself and from outside it. Bureaucrats, in other words, should solicit advice, suggestion and -- perhaps most important -- correction, both from their own lower echelons and from the public whom they are mandated to serve. Like so much in social science, the concept here is relatively simple, but it is also quite novel in that it goes sharply against the grain of most bureaucratic practice, not only in development administration but in administrative management of large organizations in general.

This is so because modern bureaucracy, whether in a developmental agency, a multinational corporation, a large university or elsewhere, has basically two urges: to routinize and to control. The need to achieve consistency and impartiality in large numbers of decisions forces organizations to create and apply uniform rules in making decisions, so that all similar questions will be resolved in similar ways, or in other words, by "routinizing" everything, the bureaucracy turns its tasks into matters of routine and thereby makes its affairs easier to manage. To be able to impose such routinizing, of course, requires a high degree of centralized control, such that officials are rewarded for following the prescribed routines and are penalized for failing to do so. Which of these two urges is the prior one is hard to say. Most social science theory would follow Max Weber (Gerth and Mills, 1958) in positing that the need to routinize creates the instrumentalities of control, but others like Gran (1983) or Foucault (1977) would insist that the urge to control is the driving force of the modern age, which spawns such derivative phenomena as routinization in its wake.

Whatever the chain of cause and effect, foresters are well acquainted with the kind of top-down, command-and-control bureaucracies that are typical of RD and forestry management in most LDCs. In RD terms, the result of these underlying bureaucratic needs is the standard project "blueprint" that characterizes most development efforts. This process is a familiar one: Once decided upon, a project is laid out with a well-defined plan that will carry it through from start to finish, with periodic monitoring and evaluation to make sure things are on track, often reinforced by a phasing approach to the funding, so that successive "tranches" are given out only if targets are being met along the way.

As we noted earlier, one common complaint about the industry-oriented, infrastructural approach of the 1950s and 1960s was that it did too little for the majority of people in the LDCs and did too much in terms of environmental damage. The response on the intellectual and theoretical side was to call for projects that would meet "basic human needs," do something for the "poorest of the poor," address women's issues, preserve the environment, and so on. In terms of actual projects in the field, these "new directions" meant that more guidelines and controls were applied to the design, implementation and evaluation of development activities. Social impact and environmental impact statements were required of projects, women's needs had to be specifically addressed, technical soundness analyses needed to be done, etc. And as evidence piled up that projects tended to deviate from plan, ever more stringent controls and "conditions precedent" (preliminary conditions that had to be met before a project could even begin) were put in to ensure that everything would move in lock step. In a word, centralized project controls became a good deal tighter in the decade of the 1970s.

Yet in fact project problems and deviations from plan are both inevitable and unpredictable, say critics like Rondinelli (1983), and the move toward more rigid planning that characterized the 1970s in fact made such difficulties all the more certain. Since project problems cannot be prevented, they should instead be welcomed as opportunities to change and improve things, to fashion better projects. The place to start, says Chambers (1983; also Chambers and Jiggins, 1987) is actually *before* the beginning, in that project planners should begin *their* work by assessing just what it is that rural project beneficiaries know and want. Most likely, it will be found that they know a good deal more than outside development professionals believe they could possibly know, and that their wants are somewhat different from what the professionals believe they *should* want. If this kind of "rural people's knowledge" is explored, analyzed and incorporated into projects, the success rate would be considerably higher than it in fact is, says Chambers.

Certainly there is enough evidence of forestry projects that have been less than successful or even outright failures that this advice is worth heeding. To take only one country as an example, Brechin and West (1982) point to a distinct lack of technical knowledge on the part of foresters in Niger, which was a significant reason for project failure there, while on the other hand Montagne (1985-86) cites a rich indigenous knowledge of silviculture in Niger that could be harnessed and utilized in forestry projects. Various FAO-sponsored studies showed Bangladesh rural households as having planted or naturally regenerated an average of 68 trees, while in Nepal the average household owned 28 trees, of which about one-third had been planted and cultivated. Similar evidence emerged from Costa Rica, Bolivia, Kenya and Malawi (FAO, 1985a: 17-18). Clearly such household activity reveals a large depth of local knowledge about trees that any forestry professional interested in making social forestry work should look at very seriously, both in terms of planning projects and of changing them as things inevitably deviate from the blueprint, once the project is under way.

Other advocates of ADA (e.g., Korten, 1980; Korten and Uphoff, 1981; Rondinelli, 1983) concentrate more on the bureaucracy itself, calling essentially for more "bottom-up" participation within governmental agencies. It is after all those working on the front lines of a project, whether in the design or implementation, that are going to be the first to notice when things are not shaping up or moving along properly. Rather than being seen as rigid blueprints that must move according to form, projects should be viewed as learning opportunities in which officials at all levels will feel encouraged to contribute their ideas and energies to correcting problems and making things work.

Perhaps the best description of this approach is the phrase "inner democratization," applied by Albert Mayer (1958), the "founding father" of India's Community Development program, to the early years of that effort. Here junior level people were urged to speak up and criticize, and the leadership of the project actively searched out ways to change and improve their enterprise (for more discussion of Community Development, see Chapter 9). But the term "inner democratization" also points up the major difficulty with ADA: How can a bureaucracy whose basic mode of operation is for those at the bottom to implement orders decided at the top actually manage to reverse itself so as to solicit criticism and redirection from lower levels? Obviously, to do so would be to run against the very inertial momentum of the organization itself.

There are instances of ADA having worked, one of which was most definitely Mayer's Community Development experiment in the late 1940s. In the early 1980s, Uphoff (1982-83, 1986a) found a good deal of ADA practiced in the Gal Oya irrigation rehabilitation project in Sri Lanka. And David Korten and his colleagues offer quite a number of interesting examples from various sectors and regions.[2] But ADA success is not guaranteed over the longer term, even if it does get incorporated initially in

RD projects. Again, Mayer's experience is instructive in that the very Community Development effort that was the cynosure of RD achievement in the late 1940s became the epitome of RD failure a decade later -- a widely cited example of a rigid, top-down, unimaginative and overextended bureaucracy. The techniques of ADA that worked at the beginning when the program was an exciting experiment no longer seemed desirable when it had grown to embrace a larger and larger portion of India's 600,000 villages. The real question, though, is not so much whether ADA was desirable in the more mature Community Development program but whether it was even possible, once the program had grown beyond a certain size. The searching self-criticism that is possible in the small scale of an experimental pilot project, in short, may just not be very feasible in larger organizations.

Still, there are some aspects of ADA the forestry departments could employ to advantage. For example, adjusting incentives within the bureaucracy can encourage foresters to learn from farmers what they know about agroforestry and to solicit suggestions from project beneficiaries on improving program management. Higher level managers can make it understood that bottom-up advice is solicited, and they can reward constructive criticism welling up through the chain of command. Projects can be modified and redesigned as experience inevitably shows the inadequacies in their planning.

The PICOP fuelwood enterprise in the Philippines offers a number of examples in this regard as to how ADA could be put into practice.[3] The initial scheme called for planting phased over a four-year period, so that the mature pulpwood trees could be cut over a similar timespan, but economies of scale in land clearing and tree planting made the phasing impractical. Consequently farmers planted all their land at the same time. Next, the agroforestry aspect envisioned in the plan was not accepted by farmers, who found that bank branches would not give loans for mixed plantings. Third, the recommended technical packages were often ignored, as farmers found they could use less fertilizer and weed less often than they were urged. And finally, the fact that they had planted their trees all at once meant that the farmers insisted on cutting them all at once on their maturing, and this in turn created labor problems, since available household hands were not enough to do the work and expensive outside contractors had to be hired. Also it might be mentioned that an extremely rare (for this particular area) typhoon devastated much of the planted area midway through the project.

Altogether, there were a number of prime opportunities for ADA.[4] Some acquaintance with farmers' needs, wants and constraints could easily have elicited the problems they would face with the phased planting scheme. And with a little more thought in the planning the project, the plots to be planted could have been phased, rather than the plantings within the plots. The bank (which in this case was a governmental agency) could have been approached at ministerial level to be more flexible in its lending policy. Forestry professionals could have learned much about the technology of growing trees by observing what practices farmers were following, and could have thereby built up a stock of knowledge for future planting cycles (one of which could have begun after the typhoon). And by asking farmers ahead of time when they were going to harvest their trees, project managers could have anticipated the labor shortage and taken remedial action.

This list of unexpected deviations from plan blueprint is probably about normal for a project in either forestry or rural development, and the suggestions given here are not merely the kind that come only with hindsight; they could have been instituted at the time with an ADA-oriented project managment. To do so cannot be easy, for forestry professionals are no more likely than their colleagues in other development fields to seek out mistakes, ask subordinates for advice or look to farmers for guidance. Yet these things can be done and if done well can turn a mediocre or failing project into a successful one.

C. Public Choice, Privatization and Collective Action

Not surprisingly with politically conservative adminstrations in control in Washington, London and at the World Bank in the 1980s, development theory and practice began to see an infusion of more conservative thinking. Among the various concepts that came to have influence in policy making such as monetarism and supply-side economics, public choice theory has clearly been exceedingly important in affecting development policy as practiced at USAID and the World Bank, and so is worth exploring at least in modest scope. This is especially so in that public choice theory has important implications for "common property resources" like forest reserves.

The theory of public choice is easily laid out in broad outline.[5] The guiding assumption that undergirds all else is that *the market* (or the private sector -- the two terms are employed more or less synonymously) *is the best allocator* of goods and services, primarily because buyers and sellers have the incentive to maximize their private gains from participating in a market relationship. In this way each commodity goes to whoever wants it the most, each buyer gets to compare the full range of things being offered, and the market mechanism acts most efficiently. Conversely, the public sector is the worst allocator, for it has no incentive to to be "efficient," whether as buyer or seller, because there are no rewards to being so, nor are there any penalties for being wasteful in spending other people's (the taxpayers') money.

The second major assumption is that *only individuals act* in transactions (groups are considered to be merely aggregations of individuals, while class or culture are given no weight as influencing behavior). Further, these individuals act "rationally" in making a knowledgeable cost/benefit calculus at each transaction, though of course this cannot always be precise. Individuals are assumed always to be acting in their self-interest, whether they are private operators or government bureaucrats and politicians. Bureaucrats act to increase their power, status, perquisites and the like, while politicians advance their careers by raiding the public till to bring benefits to small interest groups. Thus tax monies support wasteful gravity flow irrigation schemes to help select farmers, government timber resources are turned over to lumber firms at giveaway prices, massive subsidies support air travel for elites on government-owned airlines, and so on. This is the principal reason why government grows so inexorably in the public choice view, for individuals are benefiting as consumers, politicians and bureaucrats, while the public in general -- the "owners" of the public enterprise -- have little incentive or ability to monitor and check what is going on.

A third assumption is that *values are whatever people want* and wish to maximize; values are definitely *not* what bureaucrats, politicians or intellectuals decide that people should have. People choose their values in the market place, by what they consume. If people want to watch television situation comedies and game shows, and will support the sponsors of such programs by purchasing their products, then governments have no right or duty to impose "edifying" cultural shows or educational programming. Similarly, if farmers find phosphatic fertilizers useful and profitable, they will purchase these inputs at true market prices; governments have no call to distort the economy by subsidizing such commodities.[6]

There are a few very clear policy implications that flow from these asumptions. The most obvious is that public sector activity should be privatized whenever possible, so as to minimize the bad effects of government control and maximize the benefits of a market allocation -- to realize "the magic of the market place," in President Ronald Reagan's phrase. There is a spectrum or hierarchy of privatization with the private sector at the more desirable end and public ownership or management at the less desirable end. A primary goal of public policy, accordingly, should be to move commodities as far as possible toward the private end of that spectrum. If it is not possible to move all the way toward privatization, then in between the two end-points are such arrangements as *franchising* (e.g., authorizing a private firm to operate the canteen in a government office building), or *contracting* (e.g., for road maintenance, based on competitive bidding), when outright privatization is not feasible. And where things are already in the private sector, they should be *deregulated* to the maximum extent (for example, commercial truck transport or taxi service).

Advocates of privatization would readily admit that not all goods and services could be provided by the private sector. National defense or public health protection against epidemics, for example, would find few buyers if offered on the private market, because (assuming the services were effective) those who didn't buy would get the service anyway. They would thus become "free riders," who get a commodity without paying for it. For this reason, some goods and services must be maintained by the public sector (though some like fire protection might be contracted out, the terms of contract would have to guarantee protection to everyone in the region being served).

Even if one accepts the dictum that private is best, there remains some confusion over what commodities should go in which sector. Public choice thinking on this issue is best summed up by the concepts of *consumption* (whether "individual" in that consumption by any one person reduces what is left for others, or "joint" in that many people can consume without effect on what is being offered, as with a cinema or a radio broadcast) and *excludability* (whether consumers can gain access without paying for it). The two concepts can be put together to create a two-way contingency table, as in Figure 5.

Figure 5

GOODS AND SERVICES (G&S) CLASSIFIED BY CONSUMPTION AND EXCLUDABILITY

		EXCLUDABILITY	
		Feasible (market G&S)	*Infeasible* (public G&S)
CONSUMPTION	*Individual* G&S	**private** (e.g., food)	**common pool** (e.g., air)
	Joint G&S	**toll** (e.g., telephone)	**collective** (e.g., broadcast TV)

The challenge of the public choice approach is to increase the allocative efficiency of as many goods and services as possible, by shifting them into the private goods category, or failing that, to the toll goods sector. Common property resources come in for considerable attention here. To take the forest example, at some distant point in history forestry resources constituted a "collective" good like sunlight or gravity. Anyone taking a tree or two did not affect the availability for others in any way, since natural regeneration would make up for any loss to the resource. Then as population multiplied, later on in history forests in a given area became a "common pool resource," in that use by individuals did diminish use by others, for relative to population the resource had now become finite or "subtractable," in the parlance of public choice theory. Yet forest commons were still public property, from which users could not be excluded. By the 19th century in most countries (though considerably earlier in many areas of Europe), governments did begin to exclude people from forests, and turned them into a sort of "toll" good that would be sold, but only to a few people so that their use could be limited in order to sustain the resource. The "tragedy of the commons" explored by Hardin (1968) in his famous monograph of that name was averted through public management.

But not very well, assert the public choice theorists, who claim that public management is in fact mismanagement, as bureaucrats and politicians either underutilize the resource or overexploit it in collusion with greedy private interests (a process greatly facilitated by corruption). The solution, in their eyes, is to *privatize* natural resources, with the result that their owners (who are of course seeking a long-term profit) will best manage them for a true "sustained yield." Thus conservative think-tanks like the Heritage Foundation urged the Reagan administration to privatize public grazing lands and even federal forest lands (e.g., Hanke, 1983; Johnson and Baden, 1983), and Reagan-appointed commissions recommended transfer of government lands to the private sector.[7]

As can be imagined, many of the public choice demands created considerable controversy in the Reagan adminstration. This was particularly so in environmental areas, especially after the wide public attention the environmental protection had generated in the 1970s. In fact the controversy was so intense that James Watt, President Reagan's cabinet appointeee as Secretary of the Department of Interior (which manages most of the federal lands in the United States) had to resign under pressure, as did also his director of the Envrionmental Protection Agency, Anne Burford. Although it has received less publicity, there has been a privatization agenda in the development sphere as well, advocated by the World Bank and USAID.

The Bank has been pushing privatization in such sectors as transportation, communication and health (see, for example, Roth, 1987, who collected a whole series of privatization case studies for the Bank; at a more general level, see World Bank, 1981), while AID has been advocating similar strategies (e.g., Hageboeck and Allen, 1982; also USAID, 1982). Though much of the push here has been to deregulate industries and move state-owned enterprises into private hands, there has been considerable interest in the agricultural sector as well (see e.g., Maddock, 1987). In Bangladesh, for example, the World Bank has been fostering private sector involvement in groundwater irrigation by encouraging private dealers to sell shallow tubewells as a substitute for the earlier government sponsorship of larger scale tubewells and pumps, while USAID has recently persuaded the government to privatize most of the previously government-operated fertilizer trade (see Blair, 1986b). Some would carry the privatization idea much further, saying for instance that the tribal, egalitarian and "affective" cultures of Africa constitute what amount to insurmountable constraints blocking any serious economic development seeking to proceed down a socialist path. Instead, it is asserted, the African states must move completely toward capitalism as the only growth strategy that can break these cultural constraints (Hyden, 1983).

Privatization ideas have filtered into the forestry sector as well. Laarman (1986) finds USAID urging such policy reforms as privatizing state-owned wood-processing plants, eliminating government-managed marketing boards for forest products, employing private sector contractors to run nurseries and afforestation schemes, reducing subsidies to forestry investments, and in general encouraging private sector activity wherever possible.

Could such reforms work? Certainly the market does provide an incentive that is all too often hard to discern in public or communal efforts. In India, for example, the private farm forestry components of social forestry projects appear invariably to be runaway successes of individual farmer enthusiasm in terms of seedlings planted and surviving, while community plantations on common lands seem to lag behind (Blair, 1986a; FAO, 1985a; Java, 1986; Shah, 1987; see also Shiva et al., 1987). And in the African Sahel, the transformation of land tenure from communal to private property for growing crops but not trees (which remained government property) meant that farmers spent their energies growing foodcrops rather than planting or caring for trees (Thomson et al., 1986). People do, in short, respond to the chance for private gain.[8]

But does this mean that all attempts at collective action are necessarily naïve and utopian? Hardin (1968) asserts that managing common pool resources (cf. Figure 5) in the face of rising population pressure is an impossible task without very strong state controls, because each individual will succumb to the temptation to take more than a "fair share" in the knowledge that s/he will benefit from the extra helping, while the collectivity will have to bear the cost in terms of a depleted resource. The only answer, say many public choice theorists (though not all -- see Ostrom, 1986), has to be creating some kind of excludability as per Figure 5, preferably as a private good but failing that as a toll commodity.

Yet there are examples of successful communal management of common pool resources over time. Cordell and McKean (1986) describe a coastal fishery area off the coast of Brazil that has been communally managed for sustained yield for decades, through a system of informal groups enforcing communal norms. Wade (1986; see also more generally, Wade, 1987) analyses a region in South India where agricultural land is treated as private property during the crop season but then is handled as a common pool resource during the fallow period.

In the forestry sphere, village panchayats in Nepal managed local communal woodlots quite well for many decades, until the government nationalized all such land in 1957. The result was that what people had protected as their own communal property now came up for grabs by anyone, since in the local view it no longer belonged to the community. In short order, rapid deforestation ensued. Finally in 1978 the government transferred many of these former woodlots back to their village panchayats, and sound local management is again possible (Arnold and Campbell, 1986).[9]

The key here seems to be the question of *access* to resources that are characterized by individual use and non-excludability, which are labeled common pool resources in the upper right-hand quadrant of Figure 5. In the case of the Brazilian coastal fisheries, the Indian grazing land and the Nepali village forests, those inside the community could not be excluded from using the resource, but those outside it could be so restrained. It is this possibility of keeping outsiders from using the resource that makes it worthwhile and "rational" for local users to make and abide by rules of use.[10] In the Nepali case, the government takeover in 1957 meant that outsiders could no longer be prevented from using the village forests, so there was no reason for the local users to stint on exploiting the resource. Then when the forest areas were turned back to village councils in 1978, there was once again good logic in abiding by communal rules of use.

Collective action, then, at least in some situations can work, and deserves consideration as a third option to the traditional alternatives of public or private sector control. There is, as Elinor Ostrom (1986: 607), one of the leading public choice theorists, observes, a "third camp." It is a somewhat risky camp, perhaps, for the circumstances have to be within fairly narrow limits: not too large an area, not too much outside pressure and not too large a local population wishing to use the resource. If large numbers of outsiders try to move into the Brazilian coastal area or Nepali villages grow too large, their systems would likely break down. But there are a great many situations, particularly in the forestry sector, where conditions match rather well to the requisites that appear to be necessary for collective action in managing common property resources, and forestry planners would do well to look for such opportunities.

D. Decentralization

Even the most ardent public choice theorists would admit that not everything can be privatized. Local police and fire protection, for example, could be contracted out perhaps, but no self-respecting state would permit such services to be sold on a market only to those able to pay for them.

These and other services like public health protection against epidemics must be provided to all members of the community. But it is possible, say the public choice advcoates, to make community control of these "residual" goods and services (i.e., those that must remain in the public sector) approximate the marketplace by making the region covered as small as practicable (consonant with the nature of the commodity), so that local voters ("consumers" of public services) have the maximum control over their government and can make it acountable to them. Thus the public choice school is a strong advocate of decentralization.

The pedigree of decentralization as a development strategy goes back a good deal further than the advent of public choice, however, and has a long history of its own,[11] as hinted back in Chapter 3, when we explored some of the problems arising from either too much centralization or too much decentralization. The conjunction of this long history of decentralization as a strategy in its own right with the more recent interest in it from the public choice school makes it an appealing strategy today in the international development community. USAID, for example, is at present sponsoring a "centrally funded" (i.e., worldwide, not restricted to one country) project in "Decentralization Finance and Management" (USAID, 1987) that combines both these strands of thought.

Decentralization as a development strategy can be defined for our purposes relatively easily (though there is considerable debate in the field itself over definitions), in that it consists in one way or another of a conscious effort by the state to shift a significant degree of decision-making power to sub-regional level[12] institutions embodying some real representation of citizen interests. These institutions of decentralization could be elected councils or appointed bodies, though with both (particularly the latter) there is a good deal of risk that what is presented as a serious decentralization reform is in fact only a devolution of some discretion in implementation. This is frequently the case with local bodies made up of government officials appointed *ex officio* to coordinate or integrate development activities in a given subregion, as for instance a district planning council composed of all the district sectoral development officers (district agricultural officer, public works officer, education officer, etc.).

As we are using the term here, true decentralization has to involve meaningful local representation. Representation can also be an elusive term. For instance many colonial regimes had elected local councils, but the franchise was restricted and those elected represented only the locally dominant strata. And the spread of a universal franchise did not always guarantee representative government by any means, for local elites were often able to continue their dominance by deploying their power to ensure election of "representatives" beholden to them (see e.g., Myrdal, 1968: ch. 16). For the discussion here, then, decentralization refers to a serious devolution of authority to subregional institutions embodying a signficantly representative membership.

A number of arguments can be advanced for decentralization strategies.[13] The most compelling one is that decentralizing *allows a central government to find out what to do* at local or subregional level. Because each locality is unique in any number of ways (physical, cultural, economic, transportation linkages, etc.), no central government can ever figure out the precise mix of programs and policies for all places. Local inputs and advice must provide the necessary information. Perhaps more importantly, though, unless government finds out what local people want, it can never harnass their full energies to promote rural development, and unless people contribute their effort and enthusiasm to development, little will happen, for rural devlopment cannot be brought about through government fiat alone. Only through some kind of representative decentralization is it possible for citizens to transmit upward ideas and priorities concerning what it is they are willing to give their energies to. This is true of socialist as well as capitalist states.

A second rationale for decentralization is that *the rural poor can more easily participate* at local than at higher levels. The "transaction costs" of getting information and getting involved are less for activities closer to home, particularly when the participants are illiterate, inexperienced in political processes or see little purpose to participating in regional or national level politics. Another way to see this is through the concept of "access" developed by Bernard Schaffer (1977; also Schaffer and Lamb, 1981; and Smith, 1986). His view is that the struggle for the rural poor to achieve a better living and a measure of dignity is hindered perhaps most of all by bureacracy's ability to deny access to local decision-making (and thus access to the benefits of governmental activity), so that this access can be reserved for those elites who matter at local level. Decentralization should help the poor rural majority gain access by bringing bureaucracy closer to them and given them a greater influence over it.

Third, *both people and resources can be mobilized* through decentralization. People can be energized to advance social change, "green revolutions," mass literacy campaigns and the like. Decentralizing can also be a way to encourage local bodies to pay a larger share of their own costs by raising local taxes and charging fees, rather than rely on grants from higher level. And finally, decentralization is thought to have an educative value in *serving as a "nursery" for future leaders* by providing a training ground close to home. Or to put the matter in a slightly cynical but nonetheless very real context, decentralized bodies can encourage future leaders to work within a given system, whereas other avenues like student politics tend to take them outside it into more dangerous, even insurrectionary endeavors.

Despite all these advantages, decentralization initiatives face a number of obstacles on the way to fully effective implementation. To begin with, *central power may not in fact be given up*, political rhetoric to the contrary notwithstanding. Local bodies may be awarded autonomous power, but at the same time be surrounded with so many restrictions and requirements in exercising that power that they really have not been given anything. Second, there may actually be *no real intent to decentralize* in the first place; what is declared to be decentralization is merely a relocation of some discretionary authority further down the bureaucratic chain of command.

Fourth, even if some power is indeed decentralized, *local governments all too often prove ineffective* in using that power; they cannot plan, they have no conception of monitoring, they fail to keep accurate expenditure accounts, they maintain inadequate records of what has been accomplished, and they falter at raising any revenues on their own, thus remaining completely dependent on grants from above. Fifth, *bureaucratic resistance can undermine decentralization* efforts irrespective of the intent of political leaders to impose reforms, as officials drag their feet in implementation, insisting on quality control, program integrity, professional standards, the importance of technological knowledge (which they alone possess), etc.

Sixth, what decentralized institutions are able in the end to manage at local levels often gets *taken over by dominant elites*, so that the rural poor are even worse off than before when central authorities could restrain predatory vested interests in the countryside.[14] Political power, after all, is not distributed any more equally in the countryside than elsewhere, and to assign one vote to each person scarcely guarantees that all will have equal power. Indeed, one possible motivation for a government to promote a decentralization initiative is precisely *because* it will further the domination of local elites, and the regime can hope that increased elite control in the countryside will help build its own support base there in that local elites will feel beholden to it for their own increased power. Ayub Khan's Basic Democracies program in Pakistan during the late 1950s and early 1960s, for instance, is considered by many to have had just such an agenda (see, e.g., Nicholson and Khan, 1974).

Still, decentralization strategies can work, if governments have the political will and are willing to allow a long time for results. The Panchayati Raj effort in India is a success in this sense, at least in some parts of that vast country, as we shall argue later on in Chapter 9. As another example, the very concerted effort at decentralization undertaken in Papua New Guinea serves as an example of how states with widely scattered populations can effect such strategies (Conyers, 1981).

The forestry field offers examples as well, such as the 1978 return of local forest management in Nepal to village councils that was discussed in the previous section of this chapter. The hill peoples of Garhwal who formed the Chipko Movement in the Indian Himalayas (cf. Chapter 6) were in a sense insisting that responsibility for managing forest resources be decentralized to them. An intriguing possibility for decentralization is suggested by Commander (1986) in his analysis of forest management in the eastern Indian state of Bihar. He found that the claim of a state monopoly over forest rights in the tribal areas there along with an inability to enforce those rights merely encouraged pillaging the forest resource for short-term interests, both by tribals who gather by stealth and, more devastatingly, contractors and speculators who operate by corrupting the forest service. The answer, he feels, is not privatization but rather a decentralization of forest rights to local communities, which would then have incentive to safeguard their resource, both in terms of "stinting" themselves and in terms of keeping outside marauders away.

Thus we come to the conjunction of collective action and decentralization as a strategy for managing forest resources. Given the sad reality that state assertions of monopoly over forest resources have proven so pathetically inadequate to protect those resources, small-scale decentralization of a sort that encourages collective action may be a very good strategy indeed for forestry planning.

E. Farming Systems Research and the Training and Visit System

One of the lessons emerging from the "Green Revolution" of the late 1960s and early 1970s was that although the technology developed for it was not intended to be related to farm size, land quality or capital available to farmers, the larger and richer farmers with better land tended to profit from the new agronomy much more than smaller, poorer farmers with marginal land. While the new seeds themselves may have been scale-neutral, as well as the water, fertilizer and pesticides and knowledge needed to grow them, the ability of rural households to acquire these supposedly highly divisible inputs was not equal at all. The more well-to-do found it easier to obtain the inputs and know-how, for their "transaction costs" per unit were lower, they got on better with extension agents and they were much more strongly linked in with the market system for disposing of their increased surpluses. In sum, the "Green Revolution," with its international technology-generating centers like CIMMYT and IRRI, increased aggregate crop production and brought many benefits to those who were able to exploit its technology, but did little for the poor rural majority.[15]

One response to this bias was to launch "Integrated Rural Development" (IRD) efforts, in which the emphasis was to provide inputs and technology to all farmers in a given area, upgrade social services and infrastructure like roads and electricity, build local organizations, improve the marketing system and in the process link all these activities to one another -- in short, to do everything necessary to promote RD that would benefit all rural strata. The IRD approach produced some successes,[16] but its complexity and high cost made it impractical on any scale. As Bryant and White observe (1982: 290-291), the more the effort to integrate everything, the greater the burdens that got dumped on project implementation staff to coordinate. In trying to do so much, all too frequently very little actually got accomplished, as Goldsmith and Blustain (1980) show in their examination of IRD in Jamaica (see also more generally Rondinelli, 1987: 84-88).

Farming Systems Research (FSR) represented an attempt to meet these shortcomings by focusing directly on the smallholders that earlier RD efforts had passed by. Instead of perfecting new technologies in the ideal conditions of the experiment station, FSR would work with the marginal conditions actually extant on land belonging to poor farmers. It would integrate a number of fields, as with IRD, but these would be the disciplines immediately relevant to cropping activity, like agronomy, plant pathology, animal husbandry, extension and so on, not the all-embracing integration of IRD. Most significantly, perhaps, FSR sought to integrate the small and marginal farmer himself into the research enterprise, for only in this way could usable packages of cropping practice be developed.[17]

Some have described FSR as an attempt to avoid making more difficult policy decisions, such as land reform or other redistributions that they say are in the end the only real way to assist the poor rural majority (e.g., Davidson, 1987; Marcotte and Swanson, 1987), and such criticism is at some level no doubt true, but then one could rightly level the same charge against any strategy short of outright revolution.[18] If one is to work in the practicable world, however, less ambitious strategies like FSR may have some promise.

A more serious problem with FSR is that it too has proved more successful with bigger, richer farmers than with smaller, poorer ones, for two reasons, say Chambers and Jiggins in their recent (1987) essay. First, FSR naturally gravitates to the easier challenge found on the better land owned by richer farmers, where soil is better, water more dependable, drainage more uniform, traction more available and so on. The conditions under which "resource-poor farmers" (the phrase comes from Chambers and Jiggins) labor are much more complex in all ways -- poor soils, deep erosion, excessive or deficient or irregular water, bad drainage, scattered mini-parcels or land, etc. To formulate packages for these farmers is just a lot more difficult, and it is perhaps understandable why FSR has lagged in helping them.

The problem here, though, is compounded by a second one, which is the continuing top-down orientation of agricultural research itself. Scientists working in FSR projects turn out to be no more interested in learning from farmers (and especially from poor and illiterate farmers) about their cropping conditions than other RD officials have customarily been in assimilating rural people's knowledge about anything else. This reluctance to learn from rural people is harmful enough to RD projects generally, as we saw in Chapter 3, but when such learning is supposed to be a fundamental aspect of project methodology, this kind of diffidence devastates any real chance of success.

For FSR to work, of course, in addition to a correct research focus and an incorporation of poor farmers into the research process there has to be a way to move the new knowledge to potential users. As it happens the agricultural extension field has been the scene of another RD strategy, the training-and-visit (T&V) system. Like FSR, T&V also arose from a dissatisfaction with earlier approaches, in this case the community development worker of the 1950s and early 1960s, who was charged with bringing technological modernity *en bloc* to the countryside. To master everything he needed to know to promote rural development was obviously an impossible task for the community development extension agent, and in even attempting to do so this jack-of-all-trades-but-master-at-none ended up delivering very little in the way of useful knowledge to the villagers assigned to him (who were in any case almost always far too numerous for him to have had much effect anyway, even if he had acquired the requisite knowledge).

One answer to this failure in extension was the World Bank's T&V system, developed largely through the efforts of Daniel Benor, an Israeli agricultural expert (see Benor, Harrison and Baxter, 1984; Benor and Baxter, 1984). Perfected largely in India, T&V sought to replace the old agricultural extension worker with a specialist who actually knew his subject and who could disseminate detailed technical knowledge to "contact farmers," who in turn would then impart the new ideas to their peers. The system was set up to operate according to a fixed timetable, whereby the extension agent assimilates a particular message for each two-week visitation cycle, during which he visits a set schedule of villages, then returns to higher headquarters to get imbued with the lesson for the next fortnightly round. He in turn is visited periodically by his superior, who has his own timetables, checklists and messages to impart.

For such a scheme to work, it requires a great deal of standardization with frequent and rigorous monitoring to make sure all is moving on track, which is to say that it risks falling into the rigid project blueprint syndrome that the adaptive development administration approach has tried to combat (cf. section B above). The World Bank is convinced that T&V is highly successful (Feder and Slade, 1984; Cernea et al., 1985; World Bank, 1985), but others (e.g., Moore, 1984) are not so sure, holding that T&V knowledge often doesn't get delivered, or if delivered is not relevant or not put to use. A particularly weak point seems to be the lack of feedback in the system; researchers and agricultural scientists develop the messages to be disseminated outwards, but they have little interest in finding out how the message is received, much less in picking up from users criticism of the message, problems needing attention or ideas that might lead to new research initiatives. As Chambers (1983) might put it, T&V fits all too readily into normal, top-down development professionalism and is thereby much less effective than it could and should be.

Despite their problems, FSR and T&V have a natural fit with each other (as Denning, 1985, points out), and have the potential to make a very effective package in forestry as well as agriculture. Given the gestation periods in forestry, the research necessarily will take longer, and the feedback from tree-growers to researchers is more difficult (particularly if those who grow the trees are incorporated into the process), but the possibilities at both international and national level are inviting. To succeed would mean in effect combining FSR, T&V and a number of the lessons of

ADA, but similar fusions have been made elsewhere, albeit rarely, as in the Gal Oya irrigation rehabilitation enterprise in Sri Lanka (Uphoff, 1986a and 1987). Forestry should be able to do as well.

---

[1] It might be argued that categories 3 and 4 should be reversed, in that restaffing is a more drastic step in institutional change than what we have called improvement. This could be done without loss to the schema, which has as its main purpose to indicate that there are many levels of institutional change with only rather subtle differences between them.

[2] Many of these are reported in the series of volumes that Kumarian Press has published in recent years (Korten and Alfonso, 1983; Korten and Klauss, 1984; Korten, 1987; Ickis, de Jesus and Maru, 1987).

[3] The illustrations given here are taken from Hyman (1983: 29-31).

[4] Some of these opportunities may in fact have been seized by those involved with the project, but if so Hyman (1983) does not report it.

[5] The discussion here is taken primarily from Buchanan (1977), Ostrom and Ostrom (1977), Golembiewski (1977a and 1977b), Ostrom (1977), and Savas (1987). See also White (1987: 139-148 &ff) for a cogent account of the theory. The literature linking up public choice theory and rural development is still not large, but there is a small body of writing, e.g., the essays in Russell and Nicholson (1981) and PCPRM (1986).

[6] The idea of people determining societal values has some rather disturbing implications for minority rights and intellectual freedom, for public choice theory would logically have to hold that any value not enjoying widespread support in "the marketplace of ideas" (or of lifestyles or whatever) should not be kept around by bureaucrats or judicial systems.

[7] The President's Private Sector Survey on Cost Control recommended shifting a good portion of government range land (which had been leased out to private grazers) to private ownership (PPSS, 1983a), but decided not to ask for transferring forest lands (PPSS, 1983b).

[8] Interestingly, Thomson et al. (1986: 401-405) found that farmers to some extent compensated for the differential tenure status of crops and trees by informally privatizing trees on their own land: They would protect

the trees against depradation by outsiders and would appropriate part of this newly protected resource to themselves.

[9] Shah (1987) describes a variant that is somewhere between collective action and privatization in his account of group farm forestry in India's West Bengal state, where poor rural households received small grants of degraded state-owned land on 99-year leases for planting trees, which they have done on a collective basis. The land is thus individually held, but is managed collectively.

[10] Although the "boundary" dividing users from non-users is somewhat vague for forestry resources, in contrast to other natural resource situations such as that of water for irrigating a specific area, a case where it is quite easy to restrict access to those holding land in the area to be irrigated. See Douglin et al. (1984: esp. 23-27) for more on these differences.

[11] This history has yielded an extensive literature over the years; Conyers' (1982; see also Conyers, 1984a, 1984b and 1986; and Cheema and Rondinelli, 1983) annotated bibliography offers an excellent guide to it. The discussion in this section of our text owes much to discussions with Diana Conyers and Edwin Connerly.

[12] Nomenclature causes problems here. We have used the term "local" earlier (See note 2 to Chapter 6) to mean higher than household but lower than township, municipality, subdistrict or the like; thus villages, neighborhoods, communities, etc., would be local. In the present discussion, we wish to include such agencies as townships, counties, blocks and districts as well as more strictly local units like the village or neighborhood.

[13] The section on arguments in favor of decentralization draws significantly on Smith (1985) and Blair (1985).

[14] Not of course that such restraining frequently takes place, but at least there is the possibility in a more centralized setup that the state *could* defend the interests of the poor at local level; with decentralization, even that potential protection may be gone.

[15] See Griffin (1974) for an extensive critique of the Green Revolution. Other criticism abounds; see e.g., Dumont and Cohen (1980: ch. 10); George (1977: ch. 5); Murdoch (1980: ch. 6).

[16]Coombs gives a good account of the IRD approach in the volume he edited (Coombs, 1980: 1-41), as well as offering a number of case studies.

[17]There are several good explanations of the FSR approach, for example Byerlee et al. (1982), Gilbert et al. (1980), and a number of the contributions to Cernea et al. (1985).

[18]Cf. our discussion of the spectrum of rural change in section A of this chapter.

CHAPTER 8.

EQUITY AND BALANCE IN RURAL INSTITUTIONS

The twin considerations of equity and balanced growth have cropped up time and again in our discussion so far, in conjunction with a large number of topics and issues. Obviously, the two are key elements in the proper planning and development of rural institutions and enterprises. Overlooked or neglected, they are the cause of considerable frustration and turmoil, yet there does not seem to be any clear indication so far about how they might best be assimilated into RD plans. The present chapter explores this topic in detail from four perspectives.

Employment and employment creation is considered first, because decent and well-paid jobs are the cornerstone for equity and balance within a community or region. Next, balanced growth between regions is discussed, through an evaluation of the potentials and pitfalls of area development and planning. Third, the role of women in agricultural production is examined, with special reference to the historical inequities suffered by them, and the steps currently being considered and undertaken to redress matters. Finally, a case is made for forest enterprises as having special potential for delivering relative equity in rural areas.

A. Employment Creation and Technological Change

Recent rural development thinking places far greater emphasis on employment as an area for policy concern than had previously been considered necessary. Earlier approaches to economic development also stressed employment, but always as a secondary or concomitant effect to the main aim of a necessary increase in production. It was thought that employment-growth would come automatically as the direct result of increases in production and productivity, and little heed was therefore given to considering increased employment as a separate development goal in itself.

Changes in thinking about this topic were partly caused by the clear failure of earlier development policies to generate sufficient employment to absorb the rapidly growing labor force. Despite the best efforts of theoreticians, policy-makers and administrators, rates of unemployment and underemployment remained tragically high in LDCs in good times as well as bad. Concerned observers gradually began to realize that unless specific efforts were made to address this issue directly in a focused and concentrated way, unemployment would in all probability continue to rise to even more drastic and unmanageable levels.

The earlier belief that increased employment would automatically follow expanded production was based on a conception of economic reality which is depicted in Figure 6. Starting from the bottom left hand corner (A), increases in production were posited to produce increases in both income (B(i)), and employment (B(ii)). The added purchasing power then led to a commensurate increase in the demand for goods and services (C). Finally, closing the loop, the expanded demand spurred even higher production (A again). Thus employment and production both increased in ever-rising circular movements of economic activity.

Unfortunately the theorists disregarded or overlooked a number of potential break points which almost mandatorily disrupt this movement. The first (Break #1 in Figure 6) relates to production shortfalls, or times when production does not increase as planned. Such shortfalls are due to many causes, including in the industrial sector economic downturns, strikes and lockouts, bottlenecks in raw material supplies, disruption of product markets, and so on. In the agricultural sector, obviously weather must be added to the list (particularly in the tropical and subtropical zones where rainfall is so much more variable than in the temperate regions), which here would include among other things input and credit situations, goverment price policies for foodstuffs, changes in farm tenancy laws, etc. Whatever the reasons, whether a failed monsoon or a liquidity crisis that has dried up the credit system, the link between demand for and production of goods and services gets frayed and even broken.

A second break-point in this cycle is due to the presence of regressive social relations in most LDCs. The distribution of assets and income in these societies is very skewed, with only a small fraction of the population owning a vastly disproportionate mass of society's productive assets. Naturally, the return on these assets as production increases also flows to but a small group of people. The theory, however, hinges on a large mass of people increasing their incomes and in turn using those incomes to buy goods and services. If the increased income goes instead to a relative few who do not utilize it in this fashion (but instead employ it to buy luxury consumption goods, to speculate and even to export to hard-

Figure 6

THE CYCLE OF ECONOMIC GROWTH AND ITS BREAK POINTS

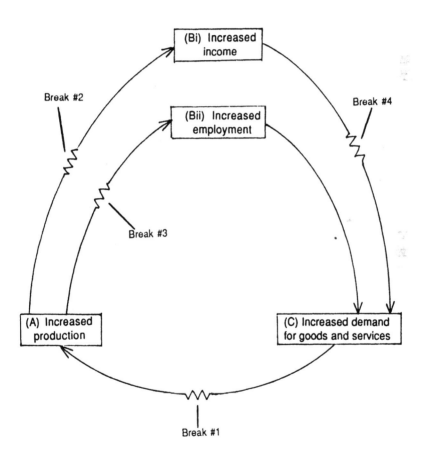

currency safe havens, as will be explained below), the second link in the cycle is broken.

The third break stems from the tendency observed in most societies increasingly to use capital-intensive (labor saving or displacing) production techniques. To do so reduces the employment effects (Bii) of increased production, because the expanded use of machinery facilitates an upward shift in product output with the use of proportionally less labor. This pattern has already been mentioned a couple of times and is treated in greater detail later in this section.

The fourth and last break occurs in the sequence connecting increases in income (Bi) with increases in the total demand (C). This disruption occurs because at least some part of the additional income received is used to buy imported goods, and not domestic products. Depending upon circumstances, this siphoning off can be quite large. It occurs because of the skewed asset and income distribution mentioned earlier, which accumulates substantial purchasing power in a relatively few hands. Since both the range and the nature of products manufactured in LDCs is necessarily limited, this concentrated purchasing power understandably turns outward, to more "sophisticated" items.

Overall, the result of all this is that actual increases in employment, even in times of relative economic prosperity, are seldom as high as expected. When compounded by population growth and the consequent high rates of entry of the labor force into the labor market, the ability of even a growing industrial sector to provide adequate employment appears much more modest than one would hope, except perhaps in a few special cases like South Korea or Hong Kong that have experienced very high rates of growth for long periods of time. In the overwhelming majority of LDCs, these break points have proven unhappily significant, such that even countries which appeared for awhile to have "miracle" growth economies, like Brazil or Mexico in the 1970s, in time fell victim to the realities of the break points and have experienced widespread unemployment and poverty. Policies emphasizing only economic growth, then, are not enough to enhance the lives of the poor, and particularly those of the rural poor. A direct attack on employment is also necessary.

This particular interest in employment led to a re-evaluation of the intellectual and policy-making approaches to a number of related questions, including that of technological choice. As a result, thinking on this subject has changed a great deal over the last 15 years or so. Four of these changes are important to us here. First, there was a re-evaluation of the commonly held belief that technology was a neutral factor in production, equally available to all individuals, firms, countries and other users, provided they had the information and the resources to obtain it. A frequently encountered concept in earlier use was that of the "world shelf" of technology. This indicated that most, if not all, historical inventions and artifacts were available for developing countries to choose from and to use without prejudice. In this sense, latecomers to modern production technology were even held to be at a slight advantage, for they were not required to "reinvent the wheel," but could instead start off from a comparatively advanced technological level.

This somewhat naïve approach has given way to a more cautious and realistic outlook which recognizes that technology is a social product, and as such, primarily benefits particular groups or classes of people in society. Thus it is not indiscriminately and freely available to all those who would like to use it. In addition, even where technology is available for use or transfer, the question of having the requisite amount of financial resources and/or bargaining power to obtain it becomes a daunting one for many LDCs. Further, it is also not at all clear that technology off the "world shelf" is at any given moment appropriate, when the relative resource endowments of those to whom it might become available are taken into account (Stewart, 1977; Vaitsos, 1979).

A second important change in the outlook on technology is that it has become clear that choices of technology are not made under ideal or pure market conditions. This is so because of the highly-integrated, and at the same time imperfect, nature of the world economy and production processes. Individual decision-makers at either the firm or the national level are heavily influenced by a mostly non-competitive and imperfect social, political, and economic environment. As a consequence, they often do not have an open choice in what they are able to do, and thus work under significant constraints (Vaitsos, 1979; Patel, 1979).

A third change in technology considerations hinges on differentiating between the process of choosing a product, and that of deciding upon the technique or technology used to produce it. With the gradual move towards a more realistic appreciation for how technological choices are actually made has come an understanding that the choice of technology is a process which depends very much upon the nature of the product to be made. This is because in the context of real production for the marketplace the range of choice is heavily circumscribed, although there might theoretically exist a number of ways in which a particular good might be manufactured. Such technological restrictions are dictated by the need to produce a product which is competitive in the twin terms of specification and quality, as well as in cost.

Thus production possibilities at the ends of the available technological spectrum are rarely considered, as they would most likely fail to meet either specification/quality or cost restrictions. The choice accordingly becomes drastically narrowed. This being the case, it becomes important for policy-makers to keep a close watch on product choices. If they do not, their flexibility in controlling the options for choice of technology is considerably reduced (Stewart, 1977).

A fourth adjustment in the thinking on technology relates to the observed bias towards capital-intensive production even in "labor-surplus" countries. This flies in the face of earlier doctrine, which held that less developed countries should and would use labor-intensive technologies in order to maximize the use of that factor of production which was most easy to secure and so cheapest for them. Studies have shown, however, that the cost calculus of individual producers diverge from what an overall economic evaluation of the same situation would suggest as socially optimal. Among the various reasons for this drift toward capital intensity are various perceived advantages for the firm in choosing machinery, such as production efficiencies (e.g., lower waste and breakages), production flexibility, a higher degree of quality control, more uniform standardization, exclusivity in markets, shorter gestation periods for start-up, and the need -- very essential from management's point of view -- to have minimum dealings with labor. The conscious realization of this shift or pull toward capital-intensive production has raised a number of important issues in the context of technological choice (Wells, 1973; Helleine, 1975).

It appears that forestry and forest-related activities have a special potential for employment generation if the technological aspects are appropriately handled. There seems to be a reasonable flexibility in determining the capital/labor mix to be used in forest production of different sorts (for example, charcoal operations, sawmilling, production of fiber and particle boards). There might also be a comparatively greater potential to vary the scale of operation in forestry, leading to the possibility of using more labor-intensive methods. In addition, even if the main production processes of forestry activities were comparatively capital intensive, there could still exist the potential for using labor-intensive methods both before and after the production process itself. This means that handling of raw material, as well as the packaging and transportation of the completed product, might be undertaken in a labor-intensive way, even if the actual production must necessarily be capital intensive. Finally, the technological ability to broaden the raw material base for forest-related products, and to more fully utilize forest crops, also appears to be considerable. If this were acted upon in a socially sensitive way, the employment created as a result could be substantial.

There is one more way in which forest-related activities could play a critical role in promoting rural employment. The failure of rural areas to develop as rapidly as urban-industrial centers in many parts of the world has been accompanied by drastic influxes of migrant populations into the cities. Those who are unable to find a livelihood on or near the soil drift to urban areas in the hope of being able to make an adequate living, if not a good one. Sadly, the reality is often quite the opposite. Instead of steady or well-paid employment, migrants find that they have to live hand-to-mouth as they did in the countryside.

What is worse, they often wind up subsisting on their wits, without the benefit of the social support they may have had in their villages, which, despite being measurably poorer than in urban areas in terms of social services, is often qualitatively better in many aspects of human welfare. From a development point of view these migrations are disastrous for the less developed countries, because they lead to an enormous new strain being placed on the already overburdened social and economic services in cities. It is therefore important for a number of reasons to devise ways of retaining rural populations in the countryside.

To do so necessarily means providing off-farm employment, for levels of unemployment and underemployment within agriculture itself are already high. There will be some additional employment creation in the farming sector as growing demand for foodstuffs plus increasing use of inputs like irrigation, fertilizer and insecticides all combine to swell the need for labor, but all these factors taken together will not serve to absorb more than a portion of the entrants into the rural labor force over the coming decades. Furthermore, most foreseeable improvements in agriculture itself seem to be on the labor-displacing, as opposed to labor-augmenting, side. Thus one cannot see anything like enough jobs for those already on the fringes of agricultural activity, i.e., the population that finds itself driven to the city. And population growth rates can only be expected to increase the numbers of such marginalized people. Non-farm employment must be a very large part of any viable answer to the challenge of creating rural employment.

There have traditionally been two avenues for the provision of rural off-farm employment: rural public works and rural industry. Of the two, the former has been used more often and longer, but studies have shown that its impact is relatively less concentrated, and besides it provides employment only for the period of work currently being sponsored in terms of road construction, canal desilting and the like.[1] In the long run it is rural industry that will have to carry the burden of providing jobs for the countryside. Given the enormous potential for non-agricultural employment generation,[2] it becomes clear that forest-related activity, and the production of forest goods in cottage-level and intermediate-scale rural industries, could have important roles to play in future rural development.

Such enterprises could have positive consequences for a number of reasons (Chuta and Liedholm, 1979; Kilby, 1982; Sinha, 1976). First, empirical evidence is quite consistent in showing that small-scale rural enterprises are more labor intensive than their large-scale counterparts (or to put it differently, small-scale efforts get much more utility from the little capital that they have than do large-scale ones, because they expend much more labor per unit of capital in their production process). Second, on the average, the income of rural non-farm households is somewhat higher than that of farming households (particularly smallholder peasant households, though obviously larger landholders and most middle farmers do considerably better than the landless), even if both categories are on average still substantially below urban incomes.

Third, strong "backward and forward linkages" exist between rural non-farm activities and other sectors of the economy, particularly agriculture. That is, those engaged in non-farm enterprise buy from and sell to those in agriculture. Fourth, rural handicrafts and cottage industries serve as a training ground for much future skilled labor requirement as industries expand, diversify, and innovate technologically. Finally, studies have also shown that savings and investment ratios in the rural non-farm industrial sector are as high as for their urban counterparts, if not more so.

All these factors suggest that it would make sense for policy-makers in less developed countries to encourage the creation and spread of rural non-farm enterprises as one part of the effort to combat unemployment in the countryside and that forestry could and should play a major role in that effort.

If this were done, forestry enterprises would be faced with a couple of sensitive issues which invariably confront all such rural off-farm endeavors. Both relate to the question of how a rural labor force can best be assimilated in rural industry so that returns are maximized for both industry and labor, but costs of adjustment for the latter held to a minimum. The first issue concerns the acceptable and established behavior patterns of rural social groups, patterns which at least initially would be incongruous with the time, discipline and productivity demands of profit-motivated industries (Thompson, 1967). If it is no longer acceptable -- and this should be the case -- for the transition to be made in the old, insensitive and roughshod ways that have characterized so much previous industrialization, special care must be taken to ensure that the necessary factory ethos is encouraged and instilled, but without the loss of the positive elements of the old ways and systems that have supported, sustained and enriched traditional rural cultures.

The second and related concern is about balancing industrial employment with farm-related production activities, subsistence or otherwise. Since forest industries are often rural based, it is likely that many of the workers would retain direct access to and contact with farms. From the enterprise's point of view this could be both beneficial as well as problematic. The advantage lies in the fact that such farm-links actually subsidize the enterprise since some portion of the workers' sustenance at least comes from outside the enterprise and, other things being equal, wages would need to be adjusted upwards if this additional or side income were lost. On the negative side, factory labor retention during periods of peak forest product output may sometimes suffer because of this agricultural link, due to competing simultaneous demands from subsistence production.

From the workers' point of view, they would obviously gain in one sense if they acquiesced with managements' desire to put their obligation to the firm first, and allowed themselves to be consolidated into a disciplined workforce. On the other hand, farm-linked supplementary income is in almost all cases very important in ensuring a minimally tolerable existence. In addition, given the volatile nature of many forest product markets, it is an insurance against market-determined layoffs and dismissals. Finally, this outside support provides an element of independence, and so of strength, in labor's collective bargaining position.

Obviously these opposing concerns are neither immobile nor irreconcilable. By the same token, however, neither are they trivial. The private objectives of enterprises seeking dependable and low-cost labor often turn out to be contradictory to the larger social goals of increasing incomes, and, as importantly if not more so, participation in rural institutions. The sensitivity and care with which these issues are tackled will overwhelmingly influence the RD success or failure of these efforts.[3]

One specific forestry concern in creating off-farm employment relates to energy. In many LDCs woodfuel has been a crucial industrial input. Barnard and Zaror (1986: 78) report in Sri Lanka woodfuel provides some 57 percent of industrial energy demand. Comparable figures for

Kenya are 64 percent, Tanzania 88 percent and even in Brazil where many more "modern" fuels are widely used, the woodfuel datum remains as high as 21 percent. If RD strategies promote a rapid growth in rural industries, where is the additional energy to come from? In a few areas alternative fuel sources are available, although in most cases only at an additional cost that might be higher than denuding the remaining forestry resource. For example, in some regions of Bangladesh there are substantial natural gas reserves, while in both China and India coal resources are awesome.

But many LDCs, as for example the high woodfuel users mentioned just above, do not have such alternatives, and for them increasing rural off-farm employment represents a very stark policy dilemma: choosing between creating more jobs and conserving the environment.[4] Some amelioration is certainly possible, as in developing and instituting more eficent wood-fueled boilers, or in promoting "dendro-thermal" energy plantations along the lines developed in the PICOP effort in the Philippines (Hyman, 1983), but this is a problem that will require a great deal of thought in the coming years as pressures mount to create more off-farm employment in the countryside.

B. Regional and Area Development

Recent years have seen a growing emphasis on the regional or spatial dimensions of analyses regarding socio-economic growth. The reasons for this are not difficult to find. The standard micro- as well as macro-level analyses are insufficient to comprehend reality, both in themselves as separate bodies of thought, as well as in their relation to each other. For example, micro-theory, which looks at the behavior of the individual firm or production unit, is hard put to explain adequately decisions on where factories get situated short of using location theory. Similarly, it is exceedingly difficult to investigate and/or adequately explain macro-level developments as they relate to matters between regions/localities without employing regional and interregional analyses. There are a large number of socio-economic questions which are not satisfactorily resolvable using standard macro-economic theory alone, such as intra-country or inter-regional variations in growth. And since such variations are endemic to almost all countries, regardless of their economic standing (e.g., the Appalachian region of the United States, Southern Italy and Northern Ireland to name but a few chronically depressed regions of the First World), a regional approach becomes almost mandatory (Mrydal, 1957: 23-38; Hirschman, 1958).

Since forestry activities are more dispersed, comparatively, than many other types of agriculture and/or industrial production, it would seem that they would especially benefit from a regional appraisal and outlook. For one thing, they are often undertaken on sizable tracts of land. For another, people in one area regularly derive advantage and receive benefits from forest-related activities that have been undertaken by people in some other area. Examples of this would be downstream benefits realized by communities from watershed activities undertaken by others upstream or the mainly urban sales and consumption of rurally produced products such as charcoal. If to these is added the traditionally exploitative nature of commercial forestry, then it would not be incorrect to characterize the forest sector as one which, more than most others, is marked by people or groups in one region benefiting from the exploitation of physical and human resources in another. To adequately assess the dynamics of what goes on here, and to suggest policies for improving things, one must turn to a regional approach.

There is also a second important reason for those concerned with forestry enterprise development to champion a regional outlook. Forest product industries are relatively more vulnerable because of the comparatively long gestation periods associated with them. One way to reduce this would be, of course, to include non-forest agricultural activities in the total development planning mix. This would not only assist enterprises at the gestation stage, but also continue to reduce relative risk much beyond that, because of the alternative income possibilities provided through diversification. Coordinated -- or better still, integrated -- agroforestry enterprises are very much an integral part of regional and area planning.

A prime concern of regional analysis is the correct allocation of spatial costs and benefits. This is a difficult matter because of the complexities involved. As we noted in Chapter 4, often there is the surface hum of activity and progress in a region, but actual development is not taking place because the real benefits are going elsewhere. Examples of this abound, but are only rarely fully acknowledged or comprehended. They exist in both industrialized as well as developing countries, and affect natural (unplanned) as well as planned growth. A good "natural" example in an industrialized country is that of the Appalachian region in the United States. The exploitation and destruction of this once resource-rich land is movingly recounted by Caudill (1962), who carefully documents the enormous benefits siphoned away from the inhabitants by externally located financiers and owners. The clear and inextricable link between the bleeding and depletion of one area for the uncompensated benefit of distantly located others should serve here as a lesson for future regional analysts. More pertinent to our interests, this economic and physical destruction of a region was not effected by coal-mining interests alone, though they were predominant, and certainly deserve the notoriety they attracted. In addition to coal, another important causal factor for the destruction of the region was indiscriminate lumbering!

An interesting example of the unintended actual regional impacts of a planned development project is offered by the Tennessee Valley Authority (TVA), which was a centerpiece of the Franklin Roosevelt adminstration to combat the great depression of the 1930s through regional planning. A central intent with TVA was to stimulate its backward and neglected region by providing the infrastructure for industrial growth, but in fact the first significant industrial stimulation was felt far from the Tennessee Valley:

> The bulk of the new equipment [ordered for TVA] went to the developed areas of the United States to purchase construction equipment, turbines, electric generators, transmissions lines, material, etc. For many years Pittsburgh, Pennsylvania and Schenectady, New York, sites of major power equipment manufacturers, received more immediate impact than did the Tennessee Valley (Robock, 1966).

In addition, the well known cases of Southern Italy and Northern Brazil, or the problems of major river valley development schemes such as that of the Tepalcatepec Commission in Mexico (Barkin, 1972/73), all stand witness to the complexities of this issue of correctly measuring the geographic costs and benefits of development. The many available examples all seem to point to the paramount importance of the element of *control* in determining regional success or failure. Where resources are located or invested is secondary to where they are controlled from, for it is this latter fact that determines who the ultimate beneficiaries are to be. Unless people where an enterprise is located have some voice in its management, they are unlikely over the longer term to have much share in the benefits it produces, except insofar as some local workers get on the payroll. Its effects for good or ill upon the local economy, infrastructure, governmental support systems and the environment will all remain beyond any influence that the inhabitants of its locale may try to bring to bear.

This is not a very difficult notion to grasp, especially for people accustomed to a world dominated by the concept of private property, but it is very difficult to operationalize in the sense of providing viable alternatives that do provide some real local influence over such enterprises. Precisely because of the private nature of economic relations, those who pay the piper call the tune. This tenet extends and applies to the public sector also, as with the Brazilian government's efforts in recent decades to develop the vast Amazonian basin without regard for the most part to the wishes of local inhabitants.[5]

Despite these problems, there exist a number of factors to which rural institutions could pay particular attention in order to advance their chances of developing regionally balanced forestry enterprises. Clearly, attention to the source of investment is most important, if not overwhelmingly so. Ideally, all investment should be locally raised, owned and controlled, or as close to that as possible. Among other things, this would ensure that both wages and profit are captured by the region, and not only the former. More essential in a sense, the long-term viability and security of enterprises is safeguarded to a somewhat greater extent by the presence of locally-owned capital. The close physical proximity of business owners to the businesses themselves tends to produce a comparatively more locally-oriented operating outlook. A local owner would be rather less likely to close down his factory to move the operation to some distant locale in order to take advantage of cheaper labor markets or more lenient pollution controls, for example, than would a non-resident corporate owner in some far-removed metropolis. In addition, local ownership often fosters a relatively greater prediliction towards non-business-related investment and support for the community.

As we have noted, there exist many examples of natural resource exploitation using capital and other financial resources from outside the region. Almost all of these without fail have worked and ended the same way--profits transmitted away to the source of capital, and nothing long-lasting in return received by the communities deprived of their primary resources, a story that is all too familiar to professional foresters around the world. Such an outcome should be guarded against at all costs.

Finally, care should be taken to maximize value-added at the local/regional level. As much processing of products as is possible should be done locally, and priority should be given to increasing the number of additional or successive levels of manufacture which might be undertaken in the region. Doing so guarantees the local retention of progressively larger manufacturing-related benefits, mainly in the form of greater wages (for the more highly skilled occupations needed for the processing) payable to area residents. But there is another sizable advantage in addition, especially if the local-ownership criterion suggested first could also be met. If more production were to take place locally, and if it were locally owned, there are, theoretically at least, greater chances of influencing the technologies used and leading them in directions more favorable to creating local employment.

C. Women in Rural Development

A significant initiative in RD recently has related to the growing concern about the role of women in the development/growth process. Previously, women's contribution in the countryside was largely overlooked, minimized or ignored. Even though in most low-income rural settings women provide a substantial amount of production labor (this in addition to their other household and family-rearing activities), they have historically not been awarded much place at all in development plans and planning, let alone a role commensurate with their past and potential contributions (see, e.g., Boserup, 1970; Fraser, 1977). This almost uniform neglect, naturally, has been the cause of a number of problems.

The drawbacks and disadvantages stemming from this neglect of women by planners fall into two major categories. First, when a large part of the productive labor force is left out of account, much of the potential for economic growth is being ignored. The agricultural research and development (R&D) field provides an excellent example here. Most R&D extension efforts are consciously or subconsciously geared towards men and through men as the extension agents, even in areas where women are the principle producers, as in much of Africa, where one finds a division of labor between women growing subsistence food crops and men tending commercial crops. Male extension workers are either ignorant of, or untrained to properly deal with, women decision makers as their chief clients and counterparts. Conversely, in many social and cultural situations, the women also are not accustomed to interacting with "strange" or "outsider" men. As a result, communication suffers both ways, and the full potential of R&D schemes is lost.

In this instance, a male-oriented R&D bureaucracy delivers less than it should, because it has not prepared itself to deal with its constituency by recruiting female extension agents who could relate much more effectively with the female culitvators who actually grow the crops. The institution does make an effort to reach its audience, in other words, but is ineffective in doing so. Considerably more detrimental to aggregate rural welfare is the second type of result stemming from ignoring women in RD: leaving them out of account altogether. Things that could be done to provide more income for rural women or to alleviate their burdens are not done, and a good portion of what is done either deprives women of income or adds to the burdens of drudgery they already bear.

Boserup and Lijencrantz (1975), Germaine (1976-77), and Acharya and Bennett (1983), among others provide useful overviews of the special problems caused for women by past development approaches, including invariably the loss of income-generating activities. A good example comes from Bangladesh, where Greeley (1982) found mechanized rice mills displacing the more traditional foot-powered rice hulling processes, which had primarily been operated by poor rural women. This displacement is rather low in the technological order of things (the mechanized hullers cost only about $US 2200 -- which of course would be an astronomical price for a poor rural family), but it is destroying a crucial niche in the economy whereby poor women (those more well-to-do would not want the dreary work) in a Muslim society could earn outside income in a way that was religiously acceptable (i.e., they used the traditional implements indoors and so could observe *purdah* restrictions). And needless to say, much of the new equipment is purchased with subsidized loans from government-owned banks. Public policy thus serves to undermine a significant part of the income stream for poor females in the countryside.

On the forestry side, the gathering and storage of fuelwood, which is worldwide largely a female task (see Hoskins, 1979), furnishes an excellent and unfortunately common example of how development efforts can go astray to the detriment of women, in some cases without the harm even being publicly noticed. Because the gathering burden is so heavily female, development activities geared towards improving the fuelwood situation should have a considerable impact on women and the allocation of their time. If woodlot projects are successful, then women would be benefited. If, however, they do not come to fruition, or their produce is diverted to other uses (e.g., poles, pulpwood) then women will suffer. It is important to note in this context that there is a difference between the last two outcomes. If the projects fail totally, the damage to women is apparent. If however, the woodlot does in fact succeed but the output is diverted to non-firewood uses, then the negative impact on women is much more concealed, though probably still as harsh. The overall aura of success of the woodlot would, in this case, tend to obfuscate the plight of the women.

This situation of failure obscured by success is in fact precisely what has occurred in a number of the Indian social forestry projects, in which trees intended by the planners as fuelwood instead were sold for construction timber and pulpwood (Blair, 1986a).

There are other situations as well where women are negatively affected, even though the project as a whole seems to be successful, or where unintended or unanticipated bad effects come up because all the ramifications had not been thought through before implementation. Day (1981), for instance, documents the unfortunate results of a rice development project in Gambia. It turned out that women were the principal rice cultivators in the project area, and that men grew millets and other grains. When the project ran into difficulties therefore, the women were disproportionately penalized and their position deteriorated from an earlier one of equality with the men to one of dependence.

Yet another case of project success at the expense of women can arise from efforts to commercialize fuelwood, for instance to sell wood or charcoal in urban areas. To the extent that such enterprises succeed, they make valuable a commodity that local women had previously gathered for domestic use as a free good, and -- given that household decisions are generally made by men on such matters -- the new market value of the wood now makes it too valuable not to sell. Indeed, such considerations may defeat the whole fuelwood aspect of the project altogether, if the wood becomes too valuable to sell for less remunerative firewood but instead gets marketed as timbers or pulpwood which would bring in more money (see Foley, 1986; and O'Keefe et al., 1986).

So far we have dealt only with some of the major problem areas of women in development, and how they might also relate to forestry. In order to complete the picture, however, we need to note a potentially very positive feature before moving on. This advantageous aspect relates to cooperatives. A number of efforts have been underway for several years to establish women's cooperatives in various fields, often with some success. For example, Kneerim (1980) documents the very fruitful efforts of the Mraru Women's Association in Kenya in first organizing bus coops to gain access to male dominated markets, and then to expand into other ventures also. Similarly, the positive experiences of the La Libertad Women's Coop in Bolivia (Wasserstrom, 1982), the rural women's credit system coops in Nigeria (Okonjo, 1979), and others (e.g., Hartfiel, 1982) would also be relevant and useful when considering the adoption of cooperatives for forestry development. Indeed, a number of case studies have shown that women cooperating together have succeeded admirably well in forestry sector activities. Fortmann and Rocheleau's study (1984) of the Dominican Republic, Jain's (1984) analysis of the Chipko Movement in India and Wiff's (1984) assessment of women's involvement in agroforestry in Honduras all attest to the fact that forestry is no more a part of the "male domain" than any of the other numerous sectors that women have moved successfully into in recent years.

D. Forestry and Rural Equity

In a world built around the notion of private property and in which the only true route to economic particpation lies in the ownership and use of some productive asset or another, the scope to expand equity must necessarily involve not just income but assets as well. Two basic choices are theoretically possible here: either redistribute the existing assets to include the deprived, or provide new assets for distribution to the asset-less. In the rural agricultural sector, where the principle asset overwhelmingly is land, the first alternative would translate into land reform. This aspect of change has historically been seen to be still-born, except under extremely unusual and volatile situations.[6] This is only to be expected, in view of the inequitable social situation in most countries. Given the key importance of owning land, those who have it, whether in small or large quantities, are not going to give it up easily.

The second remedial alternative, that of devising or creating new assets to distribute, is not of too much use here either. If we consider land specifically, by this time most of the world's usable land is either already under cultivation, or definitely privatized, even if not in current use. Bringing further new tracts under cultivation would constitute a mammoth task, involving vast amounts of financial and administrative resources, sums and capabilities which are mostly beyond the capacity of most LDCs, and where it is attempted such colonization is often environmentally dubious if not disastrous anyhow, as in the Amazonian basin.

The only remaining major alternative, therefore, is to create new assets in the countryside which are not associated with or dependant upon land, and which could be owned by and kept under the productive control of the currently assetless poor. These new assets are arguably easier to allocate or distribute to new owners than are existing resources, at least at the beginning. Even though the already entrenched interests will want a voice in what is happening and, in the longer run, will use their considerably better rooted and larger power to try and gain control of the new situation (either directly or indirectly), at least for a start the room for distributional maneuver is greater.

A couple of general RD experiences are worth examining in this context before we turn to forestry itself. The first relates to the provision of milk cattle as new assets to the previously assetless. This was done through a cooperative scheme in Anand, India, and is described in the next chapter. The second, described below, deals with some potential lessons from the irrigation sector.

Water may be viewed as a new resource in areas that have not had dry season irrigation before, and accordingly it is possible to think about allocating it in directions somewhat different from those that characterize the existing distribution of wealth. Bangladesh offers an especially interesting example in the experience of two non-governmental organizations (NGOs) in that country -- the Bangladesh Rural Advancement Committee (BRAC) and Proshika. These two bodies have set up cooperative groups of landless rural people (each of which could be called an LO -- see Chapter 6) to operate various irrigation mechanisms such as low-lift pumps (used to pump water up from rivers and canals, and having a command area of 10-20 hectares), shallow tubewells (generally having a command area of 5-10 hectares) and a few deep tubewells (command area up to 50 hectares) to sell water to land owners. By 1982-83 there were, between the two NGOs, about 150 irrigation groups doing so.

Aside from the equity aspect involved of providing some direct benefits to members of the cooperative, the groups are of additional interest beause they reveal some noteworthy attitudes in the landowners. The latter, at least during the initial stages seemed to be welcoming the irrigation cooperatives as a practical way to spread the risks associated with irrigation efforts (e.g., electricity or fuel being unavailable for pumps, breakdowns of equipment, shortages of spare parts, etc.). There is also some indication that farmers are happy to have others shoulder the task of organizing for them the receipt of water in their fields (i.e., planning and constructing channels, setting up delivery cycles, arbitrating disputes between recipients, etc.). Actually, these "transactional costs" are a very substantial part of running minor irrigation systems, and may well constitute a significant constraint on expanding command area. If landless groups find they can assume these transactional costs, and still make a profit, the BRAC/Proshika experiment will provide some very valuable lessons.[7]

Forestry would seem to offer considerable scope in this context, for it might under many situations represent what amounts to a new resource in the rural community, e.g., wasteland areas unsuitable for crops, or areas that may be forest reserve lands but are denuded of trees. As new resources, these need not necessarily be allocated according to the old distributional patterns, especially those of crop land. An obvious example is the community woodlot which, if planted on public lands, brings a new resource to the village, particularly if the land in question is of a quality too poor to be of much use for other purposes (a situation that is very frequent in the case of community common lands), degraded public land such as that belonging to the public works department, or even denuded forest reserve land that once held trees but had been allowed to degenerate. Woodlot cooperatives for the assetless might therefore be a real opportunity to exploit a resource neglected and/or abandoned by others. Individual allocations of degraded land for growing trees are also possible, as has been done in the Indian state of West Bengal in a social forestry project there. Government-held wasteland with poor soil is being distributed to landless households in parcels of 0.4 hectares (i.e., one English acre) for tree farming, along with seedlings, fertilizer and technical advice. The prediction is that a successful eucalyptus plantation wold produce as much as Rs. 12,000 (about $US 1,000) at harvest time -- not enough to sustain a household over the period required to grow the trees, but a handsome addition to family income (Foley and Barnard, 1984: 206-207; see also Shah, 1987).

Even if activities like woodlots are undertaken for the whole community rather than only for the deprived, an equity potential still exists. When the woodlots are sufficiently mature to be harvested, there will certainly be pressures to distribute their benefits largely to the richer members of the community. Such an outcome would surely not be strange or unexpected in view of what is known about village power structures (cf. Chapter 5). As noted above, however, the point is that with a new resource there are marginally greater possibilities for equitable distribution compared to old resources. It may not be easy to allocate an equal number of poles or logs to every household, but it will definitely be less difficult to do this than to *re*allocate land, or even other newer inputs like fertilizer that have already built up distribution patterns biased toward the local rich.

Another possibility which could prove valuable for those living in the forest fringes is fuelwood or charcoal marketing cooperatives. As is well known, a great deal of wood and charcoal is sold in urban areas, mostly for cooking, though in some regions industries are also heavy users, as observed earlier. The wood generally comes from forested areas, some of it legally and probably more of it illegally. There are many intermediaries between the rural gatherer or poacher who collects the wood in the forest, and the hawker who peddles it in the city, and it is a safe bet that neither of the end points on the chain gets more than a pittance from the arrangement. It can be argued therefore that in these circumstances marketing cooperatives would have the potential to provide a decent income to those on both ends of the system. Moreover, charcoal offers the scope for processing cooperatives as well. These could, through the use of more efficient technologies, reduce the huge energy loss that is characteristic of the production process and thereby extend the utility of the forest resource. They would also improve incomes by increasing value-added, as suggested in section B of this chapter.

Here, it could be argued, there is already an industry in place, with its pattern of beneficiary middlemen who will fight hard to keep their benefits. This is true in a sense, but it is also true that their position in the whole political economy is a relatively small one compared to that of the larger landowners as a class, or the bureaucracy. While they cannot be ignored with impunity, to be sure, they can probably be neutralized as was done in a similar situation in the Amul dairy scheme (cf. Chapter 9)[8].

There are also other possibilities for equity on a more individual basis, some of which do not even necessitate redistribution of land or allocation of public land to individual tree growers.[9] One such opportunity is the large number of poor rural people who do have land, in many cases a good deal of land. We tend to make an equation between "big farmer" and "rich farmer," and in an area of irrigated wheat or lowland paddy agriculture, such an equation is by and large true. But where land is hilly, soils thin, or rainfall scanty, the equivalence often does not hold. Poor people often do have relatively large landholdings, but then, of course, the land they hold is not good for much of anything in the way of agricultural crops, for if it were they would not be poor. This degraded, eroded or arid land, in many cases (perhaps even most) does have the potential for growing trees, however. Not eucalyptus that will reach telephone pole size in five years, certainly, but such land can support the growth, if slow, of some trees that will hold soil, fix nitrogen, supply humus and in general provide not only an eventual harvest, but also an improvement of the land resource.

Second, fodder-producing trees like *leucaena* have a large potential for benefiting the rural poor. In general, as one would expect, and notwithstanding the remarks in the preceding paragraph, farmers with more land also have more animals than those with less land. But when we look at animals per hectare rather than animals per farmer, we often find that the densities are greater on small farms than large ones. In the Indian state of Maharashtra, for example, in 1976-77, farms with over 10 hectares had almost five times as many cattle *per farm* as those with less than one hectare. On the other hand, farms under one hectare had more than seven times as many cattle *per hectare* as did those over 10 hectares. The disparity means, among other things, that small farmers have a much bigger need for fodder relative to their landholdings than large ones since the latter can more easily feed their animals from what they grow on their own land. Such situations doubtless exist in other developing areas as well. A program that increased the supply of fodder in a community forestry enterprise would then offer the promise (though admittedly no guarantee) of benefiting the poorer, smaller farmers more than the large landholders. More fodder should in turn produce more manure and thus more fertilizer (or fuel) for the poor as well.

---

[1] Though hopefully the enhanced infrastructure would itself encourage additional employment generation as people use the roads and canals, etc.

[2] Available evidence indicates that already perhaps 30-50% of the rural labor force is engaged in some form of non-farm economic activity (World Bank, 1978: 17-18), though much of it is in low-pay, low-productivity occupations. Thus there is a wealth of collective experience in rural non-agricultural enterprise. The question is how to build upon and expand that experience.

[3] A major concern here, of course, is the extent to which private enterprises can be induced to think along these lines (see Olpadwala, 1985, for an analysis of this issue).

[4] And if the industry to be developed uses woody material as a feedstock, as with the pulp and rayon industries, the dilemma is obviously heightened.

[5] The journal *Cultural Survival* has published over the years a number of analyses of this process, both in Brazil and elsewhere.

[6] There are a few well-known cases of comparative success in the field, such as the land reform in Japan and Korea just after World War II, in China after the 1949 revolution, or in Taiwan later on. All were the product of considerable turmoil along a number of dimensions.

[7]For a detailed analysis of the approach taken in Bangladesh, see Wood (1980); for an assessment of how it has specifically worked with PROSHIKA, Wood (1982).

[8]These suggestions on charcoal and fuelwood cooperatives should be tempered by the cautions expressed earlier (in section C of this chapter) about commercializing a resource that has been considered as free. Clearly much sensitivity from planners and project managers has to be shown in such matters.

[9]The two examples that follow are explored more fully in Blair (1986a).

CHAPTER 9.

LESSONS IN RURAL DEVELOPMENT: SOME ILLUSTRATIONS

The preceding chapters have provided us with a theoretical framework with which to analyze rural development, particularly that of rural institutions and enterprises. Here we turn to a consideration of a few well-known RD cases. Our object is to use the concepts and approaches developed earlier to first describe the projects, and then to attempt to derive some lessons and guidelines from them.

The cases chosen for this chapter meet a number of criteria. They are all well-known and established, and therefore have been scrutinized at some length, providing us as a result with as much information as we need for analysis and comparison. In addition, they deal with the full range of RD sponsors and facilitators, from NGOs through to national governments and international aid agencies. They cover two major social formations -- agrarian capitalism and incipient socialism (in the Tanzania case) -- and a number of intermediary types as well, such as cooperatives. Two cases are clear successes (Amul and Ayni Ruway), one is a distinct failure (Ujamaa) and two are seeming fiascoes that at least in one case (Community Development and Panchayati Raj) may be turning into a success, while in the other (Comilla) some few signs of longer-term success are beginning to be discernable. Finally, the five cases are geographically dispersed, dealing with subjects in Asia, Africa and Latin America.

There are of course many other cases which might have been used, some of them perhaps more appropriate for our intent. However, the object here is not so much to highlight a particular RD experience as to use it to illustrate larger RD themes. If the cases help to do that, they will have served their purpose.

A. The Comilla Project in Bangladesh

The Comilla project in Bangladesh[1] represents one of the most instructive rural development experiences anywhere for at least three reasons. First, in its early years as an incipient program it was an enviable success story -- a small-farmer oriented effort that really did work. Later, unfortunately, as the project grew, it became on the contrary a case study of how a good project could come to grief through over-rapid growth. Finally, and coming around once more, Comilla seems to indicate that in the longer term it may well have been more successful than is commonly thought, thus providing some lessons about the correct time-frame over which to evaluate projects and programs.

Comilla is the short-hand term for the Pakistan (later changed to Bangladesh after independence in 1971) Academy for Rural Development and refers to the district headquarters town where the Academy first began its operations in 1960, with an experimental "laboratory" area of about 150,000 population in Kotwali Thana (a *thana* is roughly analogous to a county in North America). Within three or four years the Comilla project became widely known as a RD success story, so widely known in fact, that a major management problem at the Academy became the handling of hordes of international development experts that flocked there for inspiration. By 1965 virtually everyone in the international development community knew that Comilla was a place to be emulated.

At the core of the project was a supervised agricultural cooperative credit and extension enterprise, nurtured and molded under the charismatic leadership of Akhter Hameed Khan, an ex-member of the Indian Civil Service that managed British imperial India at the higher levels and a former college principal. In the RD plan that he devised, activities began in a village with the formation of a farmers' cooperative which held weekly meetings and required weekly savings. When a sufficient continuity and stability had been established, the group became eligible for a loan, as well as for extension advice aimed at introducing new technologies for growing rice, the staple crop. Ultimately, the group could be granted a deep tubewell that would irrigate upwards of fifty hectares in the dry season -- a considerable amount of land in an area where the average holding was about three-fourths of a hectare.

The Comilla effort quickly achieved success on two fronts. First, it raised rice production by encouraging better practices like the Japanese transplanting methods, by introducing new technologies such as the high yielding varieties from the International Rice Research Institute at Los Baños in the Philippines, and by bringing in mechanized tubewells, which allowed farmers to expand into a whole new growing cycle during the dry season. Second, it got through to small farmers, particularly in the early years, as the larger farmers showed little patience for the slow cooperative approach, preferring instead the faster returns they could obtain by money lending, grain speculation and the like.

There were a number of factors involved in Comilla's early success, which are well worth laying out briefly here. There was, as already mentioned, the gifted leadership of Akhter Hameed Khan, the founder-director. His hard-driving and dynamic personality allowed him to get the utmost effort from his staff and to cajole funds from national-level and international agencies. Further, he was able to insulate his program from bureaucratic and political interference, and yet at the same time maintain a personal communication channel to the national level so that a steady flow of resources was assured.

Second, there was a singular emphasis on rigorous monitoring and oversight, e.g., account books for recording cooperative savings were regularly and publicly inspected, crop production plans were checked before loans were issued, defaulters were pressed until they repaid their loans, etc. Both the image and reality of administrative honesty were very much a part of the program.

Third, there was a continuous insistence on self-examination and self-criticism, coupled with a willingness and even eagerness to change things in order to make them work. This emphasis on admitting mistakes and learning from experience was unquestionably a vital factor in Comilla's success, especially when viewed against the rigidity that typifies bureaucracies everywhere. A fourth factor was Akhter Hameed Khan's ability to hold down the pace of expansion in the early years. To do so was a difficult task, for once it became apparent that his experiment was working, the pressures to expand it quickly became intense.

Against a developmental backdrop in which RD initiatives all too often seemed to wither and stagnate (Pakistan, in fact, had terminated its failed Village-AID program for RD in 1961, and by the mid-1960s was in the process of discovering that the successor Basic Democracies enterprise was not working any better), it is understandable that national leadership as well as international development agencies were most anxious to spread a workable scheme all over the countryside as fast as possible. Thus Pakistan's President Ayub Khan, the Ford Foundation and the United States Agency for International Development all urged the Comilla director to expand his project, but initially he was able to resist them successfully.

As the 1960s wore on, however, Akhter Hameed Khan was unfortunately no longer able to withstand the pressure to expand. The program in Kotwali Thana, the original laboratory area, increased its loan issue five-fold within just two years in the mid-sixties. At about the same time, over a three year period between 1964-65 and 1967-68, the number of other thanas in the program expanded from three to ten, and the number of cooperative groups similarly went up from about 230 to over 1600. As if this were not enough by itself, these were also the years when the new high yielding varieties of rice were introduced along with the new technologies required to grow them.

The combination of all these directions of expansion was simply too much to keep under control, and quality began to deteriorate. Loan officers found themselves with rapidly ballooning quotas of money to be lent out, big farmers discovered that cooperatives were a good source of funds, borrowers realized they could "roll over" their loans (i.e., use this year's larger loan to pay back last year's debt and still have a good deal left over), cooperatives discovered that inspectors no longer had time to scrutinize the books very carefully, and inspectors understood the same regarding scrutiny of their own activities from above. The effect of all these combined factors was corruption: the bigger farmers began to muscle in, control the cooperatives and steer most of the loan money to themselves. What had begun as a small farmer program turned into one that continued to deliver some benefits to small farmers but catered much more to the interests of larger landholders.

The pattern repeated itself later on after 1971, as the new Bangladesh government used the Comilla model as a blueprint for its Integrated Rural Development Program, the centerpiece of its national RD effort. In the first six years of Bangladesh's independence, the number of cooperative groups increased five times, the number of members six times, and the yearly loan issue by well over eight times. As may be imagined, the pernicious tendencies of the earlier expansion re-asserted themselves and a program that had been widely viewed as an outstanding example of success in equity-oriented rural development, instead was seen as yet another illustration of how RD programs intended for small farmers end up benefiting larger landholders anyway.

Today, almost 25 years after the inception of the Comilla scheme, there may be reason to question at least some of the pessimism surrounding the accounts of program perversion and big farmer benefit. Only one inconclusive study (Anisuzzaman et al., 1986) has thus far emerged on the long term effects of the Comilla project, but simply by noting the original Kotwali Thana laboratory area, a few observations are possible. The whole vicinity is characterized by a bustle of new economic activity. Farmers have moved into vegetable crops for the urban market, cold storage warehouses have sprung up all over the place to store these crops so as to market them most opportunely, transport links have developed to take them to the cities, and a repair infrastructure arisen to service the storage facilities and transport vehicles. Today there are a large number of brickyards, fabricating shops for making domestic implements, private bus services plying to and from the Comilla area, new rickshaw service in the villages, etc.

It is obvious that a large portion of the new investment needed to finance all this activity is local. Apparently, farmers with surplus income have not just been putting money into buying more land and money lending, as they had done previously, but instead have invested it outside agriculture. To the extent that we see here the beginnings of self-realized economic change which provides local capital to promote significant agricultural and other development, there may be a silver lining to the cloud that was otherwise considered to have descended over Comilla. On the other hand, if, as may also be the case, this increase in economic activity leads to or comes at the cost of an increasing economic concentration of wealth and unequal distribution of income, some part of that silver lining might have to wait considerably longer before appearing.

B. Community Development and Panchayati Raj in India

Anyone beginning to explore the general field of rural development is almost immediately struck by the overwhelming presence of India and the Indian experience in RD. In some ways, India seems to dominate the RD literature as traditional landowning patrons in so many countries did their feudal clients. There are two reasons for this preeminence. To begin with, there is the sheer size of the Indian enterprise. Community Development, the first major RD program, eventually embraced some 5000 Development Blocks of about a hundred thousand people each! Panchayati Raj, the follow-on program, was an equally ambitious effort reaching out to the country's 600,000 villages.

The second factor relates to the comparative ease with which the Indian RD process could be observed and reported upon in the 1950s and 1960s, both by Indians and by foreigners. The result is an immense literature on all aspects of RD in India -- a literature worth examining for lessons in failure as well as in success. Here we shall look briefly at the two major efforts just mentioned, Community Development (CD) and Panchayati Raj (PR).[2]

The CD program began in 1948, just after India's independence, with the Etawah project in the north central part of the country. Etawah itself was founded under the guidance of the American town and regional planner, Albert Mayer. The heart of his program was an elaborate extension system in which a multipurpose Village Level Worker (VLW) visited the several villages assigned to him on a regular basis, to determine their "felt needs" regarding development. A backup support team of specialists in agronomy, irrigation, public health, etc., at the next higher (i.e., block) level, stood ready to supplement the VLW's capability whenever called upon. It was hoped that in this fashion individual villagers would have at their beck and call the whole panoply of available knowledge on all aspects of RD.

In addition to the dynamic entrepreneurship of Albert Mayer, CD had from the outset the powerful patronage of the Indian Prime Minister, Jawaharlal Nehru, who made clear his own personal interest in the program's success. The program also had enthusiastic backing from others as well, most notably the Ford Foundation. Finally, it contained a dedicated cadre of enthusiasts full of zeal to develop their freshly independent country, and excited by the new departure in rural administration that CD represented.

Within a very few years of its inception, however, and despite some success as a vehicle for diffusing knowledge to the countryside, the top-down CD effort had clearly failed to provide the developmental momentum that had been hoped for. After considerable introspection and study, the government decided to supplement CD with a participatory component, in the form of Panchayati Raj, or a hierarchical structure of locally elected councils. At village level, a *gram panchayat* would be directly elected which would manage the affairs of the municipality. The elected heads of all the gram panchayats within a block, say 20 to 30, would constitute the membership of a *panchayat samiti*, which would in turn supervise the block, including the block-level officials administering the CD program. Thus popular control was established over the bureaucracy. Lastly, the heads of all samitis within a district (generally 15 to 20) would become members of a *zilla parishad*, which body would exercise roughly the same functions at the district level that samitis did at block levels.

It was hoped that the participatory element provided by PR would lend an accountability to RD which would ensure that the extension effort was effective and answered real development needs. After a few years of the new initiative, though, criticism once again became intense. Detractors argued that the program was spread too thin, that it had become corrupt and mired in inefficiency, and that whatever benefits it had managed to provide had gone disproportionately into the hands of local elites.

The reasons why these programs failed offer excellent examples of many points raised in the earlier chapters of this monograph. First, there was the over-rapid rate of expansion. In its first four years CD very carefully and deliberately grew from one to five pilot blocks, each carefully nurtured and rigorously monitored. Then in the sixth year (1952-53) it ballooned into 167 blocks, followed by 472 in the seventh year, 727 in the eighth, and so on until by 1963 it had covered 5000 blocks nationwide. Because of this perfervid pace, it quickly became impossible to maintain any coherence in the program, to say nothing of control. Mayer and the others in charge saw what was happening and tried to slow down the tempo to no avail -- the same pressures on political leaders that led to Comilla's expansion in Pakistan/Bangladesh were at work in India, unfortunately with similar results.

The VLWs, despite their meager expertise (usually a secondary school certificate or a year or two of college work, often not in agricultural subjects), were earlier able to deliver appropriate technical knowledge to rural households because each had only three or four villages to concentrate upon and a well-trained staff of technical experts at block level to back them. As the programs enlarged, however, the available supply of experts first thinned and then quickly dried up. Further, the number of matters a VLW was expected to attend to kept growing, as new fads and trends in development were added from time to time. It is no wonder, then, that the actual expertise delivered at village level diminished as the program itself expanded.

A second aspect of program failure lay in what in retrospect can only be described charitably as an astonishing unawareness of and innocence about rural class structure. There was what amounted to an unstated assumption that the Indian village was socio-economically homogeneous. Any benefits brought to a few farmers therefore would automatically be extended to all other households also, as innovations came to be embraced by the whole community. In other words, a common village interest, shared by all households, was assumed. In fact, of course, Indian villages are riven by class differences, as are villages everywhere. The result was that those who were better placed to turn new technologies to account and seize control of development resources, did so. Landowners and the educated, both groups who had dominated village life to their own advantage traditionally, came to appropriate CD benefits themselves, to the detriment of the already disadvantaged. By using their superior position, which had allowed them to dominate village affairs before, the established classes found it relatively simple to co-opt the new PR institutions as well and reinforce their preeminence.

It is in these terms that the CD/PR was seen in the later 1960s and 1970s as essentially a failure, a well-meaning but naïve RD effort that had sought to bring improvement to the rural masses, but had in fact ended by benefiting mainly, and perhaps even exclusively, the rural rich.

But that is only a part of the story. Looked at in a somewhat larger perspective, there is more to it. By the late 1970s, a sort of economic and social transformation was in process in parts of rural India, caused in some measure by CD and PR. What had happened in brief was that over the course of the 1960s and 1970s large numbers of middle farmers had gradually begun to take advantage of the opportunities offered through the new extension system. Their eagerness was considerably enhanced by the availability of the new high yielding varieties, and, unlike the semi-feudal large-scale *zamindars* of the British period who were mostly concerned with hanging on to position and patronage, these farmers responded to opportunity, produced for a market, reinvested their savings, and strove to maximize income.

They also entered the political realm, where they used their larger numbers to get elected initially to gram panchayats, then to take them over, and next to move to higher level units at block and district. In some of the Indian states the middle farmer stratum was even able to win control of the legislative assemblies, and for a brief time at the end of the 1970s one of their own served as prime minister of India in the person of Charan Singh.

Perhaps most important from the RD perspective, these middle farmers used their control of local and state level institutions to demand more from government in the way of better extension, farm credit, physical inputs like fertilizer and irrigation pumps, higher crop prices, and so on. As these strategies proved successful, so did the middle farmers' economic position, and this in turn helped to get more of them elected to office. The political and economic spheres once again served to reinforce each other very well.

The changes were not limited to middle levels only. Those at the lower end of the spectrum in some states began to see possibilities for positive change as well, as they observed what the middle farmers were doing. Marginal farmers, sharecroppers, and landless workers began to organize to demand tenancy rights, minimum wages, and land reform. These developments have not been easy ones, nor have they always been unopposed. There has been enormous resistance from the upper landowning class toward the upstart middle farmers, and from both of the farmer groups towards the newly ambitious lower strata, particularly in some areas like Bihar and eastern Uttar Pradesh states. At times there has been major violence: beatings, house burnings, rape and murder. For the most part, though, the struggle has been relatively peaceful, at least on the surface, and if one accepts the idea that some kind of social change and transformation is always at work in one way or another, then the ongoing evolution must be seen as at least a partial RD success story. New groups that had previously been neglected and ignored have now entered the economic and political arena to press their demands for a better life.

The CR and PR programs, in short, have been instrumental in promoting some positive economic and social change in the Indian countryside. These changes come with mixed blessings, and have taken a long time to be realized, but the same could be said of any substantial socioeconomic development. Overall, there are many valuable lessons in the Indian experience, including the recognition that what seems to stagnate or even fails in the short term, may result in success over a longer period of time.

C. The Anand Milk Producers' Union (Amul) in India[3]

The Anand Milk Producer's Union Limited, or Amul Dairy as it is more commonly known, is a milk cooperative in Kaira District of the state of Gujarat in Western India. Amul today has approximately 300,000 members grouped into 850 Village Societies who between them produce almost a million liters of milk per day. When it started, however, some forty-odd years ago, the cooperative was much smaller, and one of its most notable features has been the successful way in which it has managed growth.

The cooperative was started to provide marketing services for dairy farmers who were dissatisfied with the then-existing arrangements. At that time the dairy farmers of Gujarat were mainly small cultivators and landless laborers as well as marginal individuals like widows (keeping a milk cow has traditionally been considered a suitable sideline activity for widows in the region). Their productivity was abysmally low, their scientific knowledge about feeding, health, breeding and other technical matters correspondingly limited, and their incomes poor and insecure. There were no cold storage facilities, and transportation was also deficient, causing farmers to fall prey to avaricious local middlemen who took advantage of what was a heavily buyer's market, even to the point of monopsony in many villages. The buyers gave low and fluctuating prices for milk and charged usurious interest rates on loans they made to producers. Finally, other layers of middlemen customarily defrauded both retail suppliers and consumers by selling diluted and adulterated milk at inflated prices in the big Bombay market, some 400 kilometers to the south.

Amul registered as a cooperative in December 1946 with a handful of members collecting approximately 250 liters of milk per day. Through slow and patient trial-and-error experience, the scheme built itself up, to the point that two years later it had 8 village societies with 432 members who supplied 3000 liters daily to Bombay. In 1956 it had 64 village societies and 22,800 members, and by the early 1970s some 200,000 member producers were collecting over 600,000 liters of milk daily. By the beginning of the 1980s, these numbers were up again by 50 percent.

The main dairy processing plant now employs about 2000 workers. The factory turns out a wide variety of products, from basic milk and milk powder, to baby foods, cheese, butter and chocolates. The scheme has grown beyond Kaira District's boundaries to include a neighboring district as well. It has also served as a model for a national dairy development effort across all of India in the form of Operation Flood, which aims to involve about 10 million rural families in a network of "milksheds."

The cooperative can boast a number of achievements in addition to having made a successful expansion to its present size (cf. our discussion in Chapter 3). The entire organization is reasonably participatory, with elected officials responsible for the conduct of affairs at both the village level society tier and the more aggregated Union tier. The Union is able to guarantee members assured markets and stable prices which are higher than those they can obtain from private buyers, while on the other hand it assures consumers of quality products. It also provides members with all the quality technical inputs they might need, e.g., cattle feed, fodder development, veterinary service, artificial insemination services, etc. And at a broader level, it invests in general community development such as roads, health and education.

Perhaps Amul's most laudable success has come in gaining the involvement of the rural poor. Landless member households have been found to derive up to 70 percent of their total income from the sale of milk, and the comparable figure for small farms is also relatively high at 25-30 percent. More significantly, there is a heavy emphasis on participation by members of lower castes, including ex-Untouchables (Harijans). The overall organizational orientation definitely seems to be towards the less-privileged, and this ethos appears to permeate through all levels of the society's staff. Thus the organization has involved the rural poor in the dairy development process also, not just in dairy production.

In keeping with the Comilla and CD/PR experience discussed earlier, Amul's success may be attributed to an array of factors. As in the earlier cases, strong and effective leadership was and continues to be one of the most significant ones. It starts right from the top, where Verghese Kurien, the General Manager of the Union and now also chairperson of the National Dairy Development Board of India has since 1950 continuously provided an apparently ideal blend of visionary, democratic and technically proficient leadership.

The similarities continue with the strong support the Amul experiment was able to garner from prominent public people. Right at its inception, one of the first promoters of the original Amul idea was Sardar Vallabhai Patel, a regionally powerful politician, leader in India's independence struggle, close associate of Mahatma Gandhi, and the country's first deputy prime minister. Prime Minister Nehru himself was another backer, and later on Indira Gandhi closely followed the organization's doings. Over the years, various bilateral and multilateral international development agencies have also extensively supported Amul, most prominently UNICEF, FAO, and the New Zealand government. As with our earlier cases, what this level of support enabled Kurien to do was to operate fairly independently of the state and national bureaucracies, and avoid most of their rigidities and counterproductive priorities.

Some part of the organization's success may be attributed to preexisting advantages which Kurien and other leaders recognized and exploited. Among these are the presence of a dairying tradition in Kaira, however modest, in which a good proportion of the rural poor were already actively involved. Another was a higher-than-normal business acumen among the rural population there, as compared, for instance, to the national average (Gujaratis are renowned throughout India as good traders and businessmen). Finally, the vested interests and middlemen whom the dairy opposed, though established, were neither large nor powerful. Thus competition for the cooperative, though present at the inception, was not too strong, and gave way relatively easily in the face of enlightened and determined Amul activity. All this is not by way of diminishing the Union's achievement. These preexisting advantages helped in the consolidation of the dairy's success, but they did not guarantee it. Also, such conditions are easy to identify on a post-hoc basis. The credit to Amul's leadership is that it recognized the advantages while they were still only potentialities, and then exploited them in a masterful way.

Analysts have placed a good deal of stress upon Amul's organizational arrangements and strategies as the keys to its success. As we have already noted, the Union has a two-tiered organization, which is run at both levels by elected officials assisted by trained technical staff. The collection of and payment for milk takes place on a twice-daily basis (milk picked up in the morning is paid for in the evening, and the evening's milk is paid for the next morning). This seemingly simple procedure conceals a host of advantages leading to good performance. Probably most important, it helps to keep co-op members solvent, and out of the clutches of rural moneylenders. The payments also help to ensure that members have spending (household) income as well as investment (for feed, animal care, etc.) income in hand. The cooperative also provides the whole gamut of technical services in a timely and economic fashion. Since the technical inputs chosen and developed by the management are generally compatible with the resources of poor people, richer members are less likely to gain advantage through their ability to make more expensive purchases (e.g., exotic cattle vaccines, costly milking equipment and the like). In addition, the technologies and inputs are devised to be as scale-neutral and risk-free as possible, again contributing to distributional fairness.

Finally, Amul's experience as a small organization which grew in a incremental way with much mid-course re-designing (rather than as an organization which started big and/or grew indiscriminately) has undoubtedly contributed much to its success. Among other things, it has encouraged a high participatory involvement from its members, a noteworthy "learning-process" approach among all associated with it, and a strategy at the same time affording protection against subversion or capture from the outside.

Despite these outstanding achievements, Amul naturally also has shortcomings, and in recent years, as greater levels of attention have been paid to it nationally and internationally, the drawbacks have been increasingly highlighted. One criticism does not question the achievements of Amul so much as it denigrates what it sees as an excessive and unmerited attention the scheme has received as a result. In this view, the coop's performance is overwhelmingly based on the pre-existing advantages we noted above, plus other comparatively unique benefits such as the exceedingly generous external funding support it has received. These critics contend that had these advantages not been present, the project would have met with insurmountable difficulties, even for so competent and dedicated a group as Kurien and his associates.

Other criticisms offer two contentions that question the nature and extent of Amul's achievements. The first discounts the extent of participation in the membership. While admitting that relatively speaking the organization is probably more participatory than many, these detractors point to what they perceive nonetheless as a large element of top-down management and organizational control in the system. Although this viewpoint does not deny the material benefits received by lower-ranking coop members, it does challenge the claims of insider and outsider alike that the organization is mainly grass-roots in its operation. Most serious of all is the criticism levied at Amul regarding the status of women. Critics say that, despite its many achievements, the project fails to adequately support and assist women. This is doubly distressing because, far from being merely one element among the various constituencies served by Amul, women are (and have historically been even before the co-op's inception) the main source of dairy labor in the region. Notwithstanding their important place and contribution, though, women have derived substantially fewer benefits than men from the Amul scheme.

For one thing, women constitute less than 10 percent of the membership of the village societies, in many cases far less. Even when they are members, they are often found to be surrogates or have secondary status, as in the case of "dummy members" (to enlarge a single family's number of shares), or of women who are successors to male members who have died (and who are expected to assume a role subservient to surviving male family members in matters relating to the world outside the household itself). These women have very little say in the elected bodies, and virtually no involvement in management or finance-related operations. This drawback has many negative results, not the least of which is an absence of input into the wide-ranging service-provision decisions which the elected bodies make. In addition, women are denied the use of cooperatives as stepping-stones to state politics, an advantage enjoyed by many men (who begin their careers in Amul and then go on to Panchayati Raj bodies and even the Gujarat state legislative assembly).

Although they have become a bit better informed over time about the services available through the cooperative, it appears that women's basic attitudes towards such matters as caste, hygiene and family planning are relatively unchanged. There are hardly any efforts to institute services especially for women. Above all, and most distressingly perhaps, these critics maintain that the coops have not reduced inequalities women face vis-à-vis their own families. Amul's response to questions regarding women's participation in decision-making and benefits has been partly that there are many indirect benefits, and also that so long as the family is represented in some form or another, women also share in development. Obviously these are non-acceptable responses to the critics on a variety of levels, and so the dialogue continues on this issue.

All things considered, though, there can be no doubt that the Amul Dairy has made an indelible mark on dairying in Gujarat and all of India, and on development efforts in general. How close it will come to reaching its ultimate potential will depend on continued successful application of the positive management approaches that it has pioneered.

D. Ujamaa in Tanzania, by Louise Fortmann[4]

Tanzania's experiment with *ujamaa* village development is well known. Ujamaa, particularly as it is described in the early writings of President Julius K. Nyerere, is a highly participatory organizational form. Nyerere wrote of Ujamaa villages, "The essential element in them would be the equality of all members of the Community and the members' self-government in all matters which concern only their own affairs."

Such a participatory form would seem to be wholly consistent with the avowed political philosophy of the Tanzanian government. Indeed, structures for participation and communication occur in every nook and cranny of political life. The national political party is organized down to the household level in "ten-cells," which are units of approximately ten households with an elected leader. Villagers meet once a year to set development priorities and to draw up a development plan. Village representatives sit on district-level development planning committees.

But the structures often are less participatory in practice than they appear in theory. Ten-cell leaders define their jobs as conveying the wishes of the government and party to the peasants rather than the reverse. Government and party officials make decisions about what seem to be the minutiae of village life--the siting of houses, which businesses may operate, when local beer may be brewed, minimum acreages, the dismissal of elected leaders. As far as participation from the bottom goes, the development plans drawn up by villagers are often diffuse "shopping lists" of projects which do not fit easily into the financial and administrative constraints of integrated district or regional planning. The result is a tendency for village-level plans to disappear into the morass of governmental files, never to resurface. In short, the scope for participation is rather narrow.

In order to understand how this came about, it is necessary to look at the process and structures through which ujamaa and village government were implemented. The immediate post-independence period in Tanzania was characterized by an enthusiastic upwelling of self-help. But self-help proved to be neither predictable nor easily controlled, and consequently development gradually came to be viewed in practice (not in official policy) as a technical problem and an administrative task. As grass-roots initiatives lessened in importance and official activity expanded, the implementation process increasingly bore the mark of the bureaucracratic mode of operation.

The Tanzanian bureaucracy, as with most government organizations, is hierachically organized and centrally controlled. There have been attempts to counter this; in 1972, government operations were decentralized, vastly increasing the numbers of civil servants in the districts and regions. But budgetary and policy control remained at the center. Civil servants remained employees of the center, and because they were hired, fired, transferred, promoted, and paid by the center, they were, not surprisingly, more responsive to signals from above than from the villages. There was no one in the bureaucracy whose job it was to listen to and act as advocate for villagers, nor was there much, if any, reward in the system for such behavior. (And since bureaucrats often viewed peasants as ignorant and lazy, the bureaucratic form simply reinforced their natural inclination not to listen to peasants.)

The Tanzanian bureaucratic style of operation is characterized by the sense of urgency expressed in President Nyerere's phrase "we must run while others walk" and by an inflexibility which has its roots in the national ideology of unity: Once a policy has been made, only very limited public debate about it is considered acceptable. Also, as in all bureaucracies, the emphasis is on visible results. The effect of these forces is that when a policy is announced, government and party officials generally put all their efforts into rapid and conspicuous implementation activity rather than into endeavors to solicit serious popular participation in local decision-making.

The initial experiments with ujamaa were voluntary and apparently reasonably successful. But once ujamaa became official policy, it became the responsibility of the bureaucracy to implement it. Often neither officials nor villagers really knew what ujamaa was all about. But the bureaucrats were in the position of having to do something concrete. If, as is often the case in the Tanzanian civil service, one is transferred frequently, it is both possible and necessary to use techniques which will yield quick, visible results. The techniques used by many officials boiled down to carrot-and-stick approaches. Some villages were attracted to ujamaa with tractors, free seeds, water systems, and so forth. Other villages were impelled in with threats of force and jail. The former method produced dependency, the latter alienation. The result was that ujamaa never really got off the ground. Nor by any stretch of the imagination could peasants and bureaucrats be called partners in development.

What became clear in the bureaucratic involvement with ujamaa was that not only is the implementation of a participatory organizational form by nonparticipatory means a contradiction in terms -- it also doesn't work. The structure of the implementing organization in this case almost by definition precluded the use of participatory means. Participatory process is something which does not fit well in bureaucratic mode. Units of participation cannot be cited in an annual report or viewed from a speeding Landrover. Officials who sincerely wanted to establish ujamaa and participatory village government were constrained by the demands and reward structure of the bureaucracy as well as by the logistical considerations of lack of time and transportation.

The Tanzanian experience should provide a clear message for those caught up in the current fashion for participation. The structure of the implementing organization may well prove to be the limiting factor. Establishing a participatory institution cannot be a turnkey operation like building a tractor assembly plant. Rather, it requires a time-consuming process which is not necessarily compatible with the internal demands of rigidly structured organizations. When such organizations are charged with implementing participation, it is almost inevitable that something less than participation will result.

E. A Producers' Coooperative in Rural Bolivia, by Kevin Healy[5]

As in many remote areas of Third World countries, few programs during the last two "development decades" have made inroads toward improving the low incomes, apathy and low agricultural and livestock productivity of the Quechua people of Bolivia. That this unhappy past need not represent the future, though, has been shown by an organization in the Bolivian Department of Cochabamba calling itself *Ayni Ruway* (collective work). In the years since 1974 this group has forged a remarkably original rural development strategy rooted in an Andean cultural focus.

Ayni Ruway is both the name of this particular group and its system of organization and social communication. The group consists of the "external team" or *equipo externo*, comprised of five rural school teachers, a psychologist, and an economist; 12 *jatun kamachis* (supra-local leaders) and 60 *kamachis* (local leaders) complete the makeup of the group. Starting six years ago with two communities, they have now articulated a network of over 80 highland rural communities and four urban *barrios* of low income families to pursue conventional development goals within a movement of cultural revitalization. Ayni Ruway aims to increase rural production, employment, incomes, and access to lower priced basic consumer items as well as to improve overall market relations. The tactical elements employed thus far include barter, theater as a non-formal education tool, and diverse forms of production and exchange.

Barter is an institution with a long history of adaptation to Andean social and economic life, but it has been undermined by modernization forces and the commercialization of agriculture during recent decades. It is based upon two other Andean concepts related to resource management and product exchange, both of which get overlooked by modern rural development planners and administrators. The first concept, "verticality," signifies that the peasant household and community ideally seeks to maintain access to multiple plots of land (or access to products) in a critical maximum of micro-climactic and altitudinal zones within the rugged, mountainous Andean terrain. This practice offers them a more diversified food basket by seeking to incorporate the sharp contrasts in crop potential among climactic zones. "Reciprocity," the second concept, involves symmetrical patterns for the exchange of goods, gifts, and labor services between families, kinship groups and communities without middlemen or markets.

Ayni Ruway links together communities in diverse ecological zones through a chain of *pirwas* (strategically located storage-exchange centers) and *ayni wasis* ("houses for everyone") managed by the kamachi. Each community joins the network by endorsing the basic principles of social communications and by offering a specific product (e.g., wheat, wool, freeze-dried potatoes) for which demand exists and whose exchange value gives access to a variety of basic consumer items which are also locally produced (e.g, candles, soap, noodles, hats, sugar, salt). To produce these non-farm products for the Ayni Ruway network, small cottage industries have been organized in ayni wasis in urban Cochabamba. Exchange values for all these items are set regularly by an assembly of kamachis, jatun kamachis and members of the "external team" of educators; there is no cash involved in these transactions. Overall, the network constitutes an alternative rural development strategy to satisfy some basic needs and to minimize the prevailing unequal market relations of rural communities with the outside world.

It should be noted, however, that not all members of affiliated communities participate in Ayni Ruway (an estimate would be on the order of 40-60 percent) nor has Ayni Ruway totally replaced the market with the barter mechanism. Its barter system presently functions in terms of a limited number of priority products for the farm households, which have been the easiest to produce technologically and/or the easiest to acquire and transport in bulk. Nonetheless, self-reliance remains a long term goal and measurable advances toward it are made each year.

Handicrafts production is the single profit-making activity built into the non-monetary exchange network. Over 450 artisans in rural communities make ponchos, bags, scarfs, alpaca, fabric, etc., to be sold by Ayni Ruway's urban commercial outlet, PROCAM. Some of this diverse production gets exported to Western Europe, but the major volume passes to tourists and internal middle- and upper-class markets. The artisans are rural-based and exchange their products at the local pirwa to obtain the basic consumer items flowing through the network channels. As its retail outlet, PROCAM gives a cash flow to the Ayni Ruway system for incremental capital accumulation, savings and the capacity to invest (redistribute) earnings in the expanding urban and rural productive and social infrastructure. The jatun kamachis participate by taking turns handling specific administrative functions in bookkeeping, accounting, banking, and investment decisions in PROCAM.

The Ayni Ruway system displays an interesting blend of centralized and decentralized decision-making functions in a non-bureaucratic setting. The equipo externo members are stationed three-quarters of the time in rural communities and the rest in Cochabamba with PROCAM. There are no centralized officers, a difference from most rural development agencies. The equipo works closely with the jatun kamachis in administration of grant monies, quality control of the handicrafts products, the PROCAM handicraft business, co-ordination of transport, production, technical training of the kamachis and in the reinvestment of earnings in productive and social-cultural infrastructure. For informalized decision-making, however, there is a great deal of interaction with the kamachis administering the ayni wasis and pirwas, to the extent that in many cases it is difficult to pinpoint who actually makes a given decision.

Forty-eight out of fifty-eight kamachis are young Quechua women in their teens and twenties. This is partly explained by the nature of exchange and handicrafts activities, which are traditionally in the domain of Andean women, and because of the seasonal out-migration of many male heads of farm households in an area of acute agricultural underemployment. Kamachis are not elected formally by the community. Instead, they volunteer themselves after demonstrating a commitment to action endorsed by Ayni Ruway principles. The jatun kamachis and the "external team" approve their self-selection, once support, dedication and ability have been ascertained. This widespread presence of young women in local leadership positions in the movement undoubtedly helps reduce the "bossism" syndrome which still plagues *campesino* syndicate organizations elsewhere in Latin America.

Along with the organization and institutionalization of the barter mechanism, Ayni Ruway motivates rural participation by using a repertoire of activities which revitalize Quechua language, culture, values and history. Perhaps the foremost concern is upgrading the status of the mother tongue, Quechua, which has historically been second class compared with Spanish and systemically suppressed by the state since the European invasion centuries ago.

One good example is the rapid proliferation of theater groups within the community network. Over 15 kamachi-organized theater groups involving 70 people perform dramas on a regular basis with themes such as rural-urban conflicts, declining ritual practices, problems with merchants, truck-owners, local bosses, and schoolteachers, and the superior shared values espoused within Ayni Ruway. Another activity is publishing a Quechua newspaper which chronicles current events, and retells popular stories. The newspaper is written in the community by Ayni Ruway members, printed by the "external team" in the city and then returned to the community for distribution and discussion as the official organ of popular cultural expression.

In sum, the Ayni Ruway network has extended into wool-producing Quechua speaking areas of northern Argentina and Bolivia, among some of the most traditional and isolated ethnic groups generally outside the mainstream of rural development programs and projects. In these areas, where cultural continuities are so deeply embedded and protected, Ayni Ruway can be expected to generate another fascinating chapter in the Latin American rural development experience.

[1] The themes developed here are explored in more detail in Blair 1978, 1982.

[2] This section is condensed from Blair (1982).

[3] This section draws heavily upon Gettens (1982) in general, and in particular upon Mazumdar (undated) for the review of women's issues. Also used are Somjee and Somjee (1978), Paul (1982) and Korten (1980).

[4] This section by Louise Fortmann is reprinted from the *Rural Development Participation Review* 1, 1 (Summer 1979). It is condensed from a longer study (Fortmann, 1980).

[5] This section by Kevin Healy is condensed from his essay in the *Rural Development Participation Review* 1, 3 (Spring 1980).

PART IV

FITTING FORESTRY AND RURAL DEVELOPMENT TOGETHER

Today, after long isolation from the agricultural sector and the wider sphere of activity that has come in recent decades to be known as rural development, forestry and particularly social forestry have taken on similar concerns: working with peasant communities, improving the lot of the poor rural majority and increasing aggregate rural incomes. Given the longer experience of rural development practice and theory in working this terrain, it follows that there are a good number of valuable lessons for forestry in the overall RD experience, which will become increasingly worth knowing as development planners, international donors and host-country governments seek to make forestry a more integral part of their total RD enterprise. Many of these lessons relate to successful approaches and strategies that might be adopted by forestry for its own needs and agendas, and these positive experiences were the central focus of Part III. But there are also specific cautions distilled from the RD experience that need to be heeded if unnecessary pitfalls are to be avoided.

Chapter 10 begins with an analysis of some of the more important pitfalls that may lie ahead for forestry as it finds itself becoming more and more integrated into RD. We then go on in Chapter 11 to draw some conclusions emerging from our examination of the RD experience that we think will be most useful for planners and administrators in development forestry.

CHAPTER 10.

POTENTIAL PITFALLS FOR FORESTRY IN DEVELOPMENT

As should be clear from previous chapters, we see a multitude of obstacles, roadblocks and hurdles in the way of rural development that are relevant to forestry. We have tried to analyze and illustrate these constraints in some detail, as well as strategies to circumvent and surmount them. In this chapter we focus on four pitfalls that we see as particularly germane to development forestry and which can serve as a summary of what we have examined earlier at greater length. We hope that readers in the forestry field will gain some new and useful insights from each of our chapters, but, if there is anything especially that we want them to carry away from our book as knowledge about traps to avoid in development planning and administration, it is the concerns that we lay out here.

A. "Building on the Best" as an Extension Strategy

Most of the extension community's attention in RD has been directed towards those farmers who are interested in innovation and willing to take risks. These individuals are regarded as "progressive farmers," and in many ways it makes sense for a government extension service to aim its efforts at them. For one thing, time and personnel are severely limited. There are never enough qualified extension agents to go around, and most of them are overworked if they do their jobs conscientiously. Given that there always seem to be too many farmers to cover and not enough time to do so, what better strategy than to work with those most likely to respond favorably? It is because of realities like this that the target group so regularly turns out to be the more educated farmers, those more open to new ideas, amenable to change, and willing to take risks. A second issue has to do with the pace of adoption. Usually the best way for an extension agent to demonstrate success to his supervisor is to show a high rate of adopters for whatever practice he is supposed to be promoting at the moment. Career advancement rewards, in other words, come more readily from working with the most receptive farmers.

Third, and more importantly from the national policy viewpoint, there is great interest in getting food production up as quickly as possible. Hence those most eager to try new methods are sought out, encouraged and (all too often) even subsidized, so that there is a quick demonstration effect. The assumption is that once the new technologies have been proven, they will take hold with even the more cautious and traditional farmers.

The drawback to this approach of course is that the "progressive" farmer is also generally the rich one. This is the person with more education to apply, more land to experiment with and more surplus income to provide a cushion against the risks of a new technology. Then if the new technology works, the entrepreneurial "risk-takers" get a head start on their less fortunate competitors and improve their relative position even further. In other words, technological change, if disseminated through the quickest and easiest extension approach possible, invariably tends to exacerbate the already unequal socio-economic structure in the countryside (see, e.g., Saint and Coward, 1977).

An excellent example of the wealthy doing well in social forestry is Kalidas Patel, the famous model farm forester in central Gujarat (he is the one whom foreign consultants and visiting dignitaries are taken to see), who was one of the very first to devote his land to farm forestry in a big way. Altogether he planted some fifty hectares of irrigated land in eucalyptus, and by 1978 an outside financial analysis showed Patel to be earning an internal rate of return of 36 percent annually on his investment (including imputed land value -- excluding the land, which he presumably had held for many years and thus was not an item of cost for him, the rate of return was 129 percent per annum; see Karamchandani, 1982: 103ff).

Kalidas Patel has been most successful in building up a business in producing construction poles and timbers. His operation is a model of efficiency, and his income must be the envy of all who know him. Sure enough, there has been a significant spread of this technology downward through the income strata, but laws of supply and demand dictate that by the time the small and marginal farmers sell their poles, prices on the local market will not be so high as when Patel and the early pioneers in the field had the lion's share of the trade.

There is a balance then between strategies that "build on the best," getting quicker results of a sort by widening the gap between rich and poor, and other approaches that reach more evenly across the whole social spectrum to "build on the rest," albeit in slower and less spectacular ways. The realities of political and administrative pressure that most agencies in developing countries find themselves under favor the first strategy, and the

Kalidas Patel model will be a tempting one to those charged with implementing farm forestry projects. We do not want to say that it is wrong to work with responsive, "progressive" farmers, but it must be kept in mind that to do so exclusively or even principally will almost certainly exacerbate rather than reduce income differences in the countryside. More attention must be devoted to "building on the rest," if social forestry is to deliver on its promise to improve the lot of the poor rural majority.

B. Cash-cropping Biomass at the Expense of Food Crops

An especially distressing problem in RD has been the tendency for successful cash crops to displace staple food crops, and the people who grow them as well. For example, this has happened in the 1970s with groundnuts in the West African Sahel (Franke and Chasin, 1980; also ICIHI, 1986: 59-61), and over a longer period with cotton and beef cattle raising in Central America (Durham, 1979; Dorner and Quiros, 1973; Williams, 1986). The common pattern is for an export activity to move into an area, buy out or evict peasant farmers from the best land, and set up operations on large scale estates, which are generally much more mechanized. In the process, the "luckier" displaced peasants are hired as wage laborers in the new operation and may be settled on more marginal land to grow a small subsistence crop,[1] while those less fortunate are thrown out of land and employment altogether.

The new work force becomes subject to the vagaries of the international commodities market for its own jobs, and so often finds itself under- or unemployed as world commodity prices fluctuate up and down. In such circumstances, their marginal lands (if they are lucky enough to have any) are far from adequate to provide full subsistence, and much suffering ensues. From the RD point of view, the whole process becomes a retrogression, and, in some cases such as the Sahel, a very severe one as rural poverty increases rather than decreases.

National planners justify this sort of "development" by pointing out the crying need for foreign exchange in most LDCs. Given a country's (always strong) demand for hard currency and its normally very limited export base, government is forced to turn to the only products it has or can begin to produce in its bid to earn exchange, even if it is clearly aware of the repercussions that such export strategies will have on the rural poor. Critics of export agriculture argue that there are better ways to grow export crops, ones which do not push peasants aside, but instead include them in the development of the new activity as full participants rather than merely as casual sometime day-laborers. However, this is easier said than done, particularly in view of the structural and system constraints we have discussed in this book. Equally unlikely is the chance that elites can be persuaded or coerced into cutting down on the luxury imports that impose so much of the foreign exchange burden in many LDCs.

And when all this is combined with the pattern of capital flight that leads nervous (or greedy) national elites to export their liquid capital to the point that in some cases more exchange is leaving the country than is coming in through foreign aid and bank loans, the picture can be bleak indeed. There are no easy answers to these dilemmas, which is precisely why the Third World today is in the midst of an unprecedented debt crisis. Forestry is only a minor actor in this drama, and its exports are only a small part of the total for all but very few countries, so it is not a major culprit here on the order of cotton, cattle or ground nuts, but the pattern of food crop displacement that we have described here is one that forestry planners should keep firmly in mind as they get called upon by national ministries to contribute their share toward earning foreign exchange.

Problems with forestry displacing food crops have emerged on a national level in some cases, as is evidenced by the growing controversy over eucalyptus farm forestry in South India. Karnataka state's social forestry project has been a great success in terms of trees planted, both on private holdings and on government lands. The vast bulk of this planting has been in eucalyptus, virtually all of which has gone to the paper and rayon industries. Much of the land for these trees, however, has come from food crops, as bigger farmers have converted their land to the more profitable tree crops. There is even some indication that this practice has driven subsistence farmers unwillingly to switch to eucalyptus, inasmuch as trees of that species planted on land adjacent to their plots suck up so much water from their food crops that the only recourse is to retaliate by planting eucalyptus themselves.[2]

Thus social forestry has taken land out of food production and depressed the demand for rural labor (since the trees require less labor than food crops). Ironically and perversely, social forestry even *contributes* to deforestation by substituting eucalyptus for other trees (particularly on government land that has been devoted to social forestry) that had previously provided fodder and fuelwood. Animals will not eat eucalyptus leaves, and the wood burns too hot and fast for most domestic cooking, so when it replaces more traditional species, rural households find themselves putting more pressure on the diminished non-eucalyptus species that they can use to meet their needs. (Chandrashekhar et al., 1987; also Shiva et al., 1982 and 1987; and Alvares, 1982).

On the other hand, India's economy of 800 million people is a growing one, in which demand for rayon and paper is inexorably increasing. One recent estimate, for example, holds that newsprint demand will rise from 260 thousand metric tons in 1981 to 430 ten years later and then to 720 by year 2000 -- roughly a tripling in two decades (Agarwal and Narain, 1985: 72). Unless newpapers, magazines and other users of newsprint are to be repressed by cutting down on their supplies, this growing demand must somehow be met, either by domestic production or by imports. Inasmuch as India appeared by the early 1980s not merely to have become self-sufficient in foodgrains but even to have built up a considerable buffer stockpile,[3] it may well make sense at the policy planning level to work on import substitution strategies for producing newsprint.

The point here, then, is not that cash crops like trees should never be substituted for food crops, but that any decision to do so must be made extremely carefully, whether the end in view is foreign exchange earnings or production for a domestic market. To implement a social forestry scheme necessarily means not to do something else, and these opportunity costs must be weighed with great delicacy and care.

C. Shrinking Employment Rather than Providing It

The problem of public policy decreasing food production carries over into the employment sector as well. It is well known that what is good for an individual or a particular firm may not be good for society at large, and vice versa. Because of the private nature of cost/benefit calculation that individuals and firms make, though, social disadvantages or debits are rarely factored in. Thus an industry polluting a nearby water source as part of its manufacturing process has customarily treated these costs to society as "externalities" to itself, since (until quite recently anyway) it has not been required to reimburse society for the environmental damage it causes. Such costs are only "internalized" in the firm's cost/benefit calculus if society decides to charge the firm with them. In the pollution example, this would happen if anti-pollution devices were mandated, tax assessments levied to build and utilize a sewage treatment facility in the public sector, or clean-up charges imposed against the offending industry.

In the case of export agriculture, the private cost calculus of individual producers may well favor cash crops over staples. Their calculations can go this way because cash crops have a higher value in their own right on the international market or (more likely today as governments find themselves strapped to earn foreign exchange) because the export cash crops are subsidized by government in order to encourage production. In either case the price to the individual producer is higher than for growing staples, and so the benefits of producing for export are thereby "privatized". The social costs in terms of decreased subsistence production and rural employment, however, are not paid by the cash crop producer but rather by the marginal farmer and agricultural laborer who finds him/herself unemployed, as bigger farmers maximize profits from the new crops by squeezing smaller farmers and sharecroppers off the land and replacing hand labor with more "efficient" and easily managed machines (or in the case of beef cattle and trees moving to commodities that inherently require less labor input).

These problems are compounded in RD because employment generation as a public policy matter is clearly not considered to be a private concern, and accordingly it does not figure in planning at the level of the individual firm or farm. On the contrary, it might be argued that if anything *employment reduction* is a goal of business at the micro-level (Olpadwala, 1985). This is because labor is a major if not principal cost factor for many businesses, in terms of both actual wages and the management energy needed to deal with strikes, worker demands, plant disruptions and the like. The result is the trend toward mechanization and less labor-intensive commodities noted just above. Private employers gain but the greater public may well lose, as jobs dry up.

As we have seen, forestry is scarcely immune from these considerations, especially the types of farm forestry that have been promoted in India and other countries. Public policy in such projects as farm forestry may very well serve to shrink employment opportunities rather than enlarge them. To do so may be a tradeoff that planners and political decision-makers are willing to undertake, given their priorities and assessments of where the greatest societal needs lie, as we outlined at some length for the case of eucalyptus farming in the previous section. But these decisions cannot be taken lightly and must only be taken in full knowledge of the consequences for rural employment. It will not do to ignore or dismiss the employment consequences of forestry programs by pointing to hopeful estimates of downstream employment generation in wood processing, marketing and use while forgetting that the very production of the wood itself may be costing society far more in the way of employment foregone.

D. People, Government and the Legacy of History

The problem of transforming forestry services from regulatory agencies to RD extension organizations is a topic frequently encountered in forestry circles in recent years. It is often depicted in terms of turning forest guards into extension agents, or changing policemen into salesmen, and is rightly considered a difficult goal to achieve, albeit one well worth striving for.

The roots of the matter go far deeper than forestry, though, and extend far beyond the forest sector. Rural people have long distrusted government, mostly for good reason, as historically its relation to the rural citizenry has been substantially one of overseer and distant feudal lord, who extracted taxes and maintained some semblance of order in the countryside. In both functions it generally was capricious and uneven, functioning through processes characterized by favoritism, corruption and a bias of privilege toward locally dominant elites, who helped the government raise its tax money (not of course by paying taxes itself but rather by assisting in extracting a surplus from the lower rural orders) and keep the peace in return for being guaranteed continuity in its dominance and a share of the rural surplus that it was helping to cream off. This legacy, particularly in the form of corruption, has continued down to present times (e.g., Scott, 1972), as for example in irrigation, where rampant corruption continues to debilitate both efficiency and the relationship between government and citizenry (see Wade, 1982 for a case study).

For RD efforts the consequences of this legacy are severe. Why should a peasant participate heavily in an RD extension package being promoted by government if he expects -- and quite reasonably so, given past experience -- that crucial inputs will be siphoned off through corruption before they get to him? And if the peasant producer is a female, as in so much of Africa, why should she think that the extension agents are going to give her any time for some new program, when they have never done so with previous programs? Parallel problems of short bureaucratic attention spans and inefficiency are also another part of this legacy. The agriculturist being "sold" a T&V extension package will still be there years later, trying to make a living from farming, but there is no guarantee that the project will be around even after a couple of years. Further, even if the project is there, even if it is still in place, can and will it deliver the goods? Who will supply spare parts for water pumps, distribute insecticides and pesticides to combat the blights that new and genetically vulnerable crop varieties are subject to, backstop financing, and so on? Third World farmers know only too well from bitter experience the incompetence, inefficiency, corruption and inconstancy that politicians and administrators are susceptible to everywhere.

This is the context, then, in which forestry finds itself when commencing its own developmental efforts and programs. Not only must it deal with the residue of its own past record in relating to rural people, but it must also contend with the often unfortunate consequences that the same people have suffered in recent decades from misguided and bungled RD projects and have endured earlier at the hands of extractive colonial (as well as independent) governments. Accordingly, it is easy to understand why villagers find it difficult to believe that village woodlots will really ever belong to them, forestry department protestations notwithstanding, or that official support for recommended innovations will not suddenly disappear, or that local elites will not somehow make off with all the proceeds of a project that has been touted as a "community" undertaking. Successes in RD or the sort we have analyzed in this book constitute a wealth of experience that can be most useful to forestry development efforts, but at the same time the more numerous RD failures have in a very real sense fouled the developmental nest and have made it that much harder for forestry enterprises to succeed.

The need to transform this kind of distrust into a sense of faith in government is immense and daunting, both for forestry as well as for the RD enterprise as a whole. Yet, it is absolutely necessary to do so if forestry is to become a successful component of rural development, and concerted efforts to effect such a transformation must be included as a fundamental part of social and community forestry activities.

---

[1]In permitting those receiving the land to grow some food for their households, this arrangement conveniently allows their new employers to pay them a lower wage than would be necessary for urban workers, who generally must provide for their families entirely from wages (though certainly not always; often urban workers also leave families in their home villages and remit part of their wages home to provide in part for family

subsistence, thereby in effect giving the same subsidy to their urban employers by accepting lower pay).

[2]The controversy over eucalyptus has become an intense one, to the extent that the FAO Forestry Department apparently felt obligated to do a study on its ecological effects (FAO, 1985a: esp. 1-2). On the issue of small farmers finding themselves forced to grow eucalyptus, see Chandrashekhar et al. (1987)

[3]Though to be sure the vast problem of assuring an equitable distribution of that foodgrain production remained to be dealt with.

CHAPTER 11. CONCLUSION

In this book we have dealt with a multitude of rural development issues spread over a range of topics. In doing so, we first focused on some of the major obstacles to rural progress, then went on to outline various ways of overcoming these barriers. On the conceptual side, we analyzed local organizations as a vehicle for promoting RD, as well as several specific strategies that have been employed in RD efforts, often with considerable success. In addition, we examined some of the effects RD efforts have had on equity and balance in the countryside, particularly in terms of employment creation, regional development, women's roles and income/wealth distribution. On the practical side, we (with the help of our colleagues Louise Fortmann and Kevin Healy) examined a number of prominent RD experiences from different areas of the world for lessons and clues about what might be copied and/or avoided. Throughout the book we have taken care to link each issue being considered to the various types of resource, organization, policy, and structural-systemic constraints identified at the outset. And as we went along, we endeavored to relate the discussion to the forestry sector as much as possible.

In the process a number of patterns emerged. First, it became abundantly clear as we proceeded that *RD and forestry share a common environment* -- not only the geophysical one of the rural countryside, but also and more importantly, the socio-economic one of common structural and system constraints. The major constraints upon development in RD are paralleled and replicated in the forestry sector, in particular an egregiously biased distribution of productive assets and income, a proclivity among development specialists to work with those already advantaged and better off, and a pronounced tendency for all manner of development programs to be co-opted by these same rural elites in good time, even when the specific intent of the programs is to assist those at the lower end of the rural social ladder.

Second, and no less important, the book throughout presented strong evidence for and advocated *people's participation* in the development process. The central role of participation from all elements in rural society cannot be overstressed, not just in obvious terms of benefits, but also in the research process, project planning and design, implementation, evaluation and feedback, and efforts to modify projects as they move along. Indeed, if there was one common element or link running through all our analyses, it has been the key importance of encouraging all rural people to take a maximum hand in controlling their own destiny.

Participation is greatly facilitated through *local organizations*, which form a third theme. LOs can avoid both the debilitating rigidities of the public sector and the self-seeking greed of the private sector, while at the same time enjoying the accountability of a membership-based institution that answers to a local audience.

Also closely linked to participation was, fourth, the need to employ an *adaptive development administration approach* in all development activity, both RD and forestry, project-related or otherwise. Such an orientation allows a project to profit not only from the energy, enthusiasm and perspicacity of its entire staff who will feel encouraged to offer constructive criticism and suggestion, but also from intended project beneficiaries who will likewise find an atmosphere receptive to their taking an active role. Among other things, projects could better incorporate the often profound background knowledge that local people already possess about specific activity to be taken up, they could more easily expand from pilot status to full scale, their research and extension systems would become better linked together and more effective, they could cover a larger proportion of their "target populations," and their benefits would be more evenly distributed. Development activities would be better designed to begin with, but more importantly would be better able to respond to the inevitable snags and setbacks that attend all human undertakings.

Fifth, the book has pointed to the importance of *decentralization* in designing and implementing development projects, so as to take maximum advantage of local knowledge and resources, also to permit maximum flexibility in dealing with local peculiarities of physical, cultural and socio-economic environment. Also in the bargain, decentralization brings development activity much closer to its "consumers", allowing them increased voice in its management. And with common pool resources such as communal woodlands, the possibility of *resource management through collective action* becomes a real possibility, in which local people can control the use (and abuse) of resources that otherwise would diminish and disappear altogether under increasing population pressures.

Sixth and finally, we noted in several places the critical importance of adopting a *medium-to-long-term outlook* in conceiving and implementing development projects. Social change is always a long (and from the vantage point of the instigators often a tedious) process, and attention must be paid to providing it an adequate time horizon in which to take place. Otherwise, frustrations and disappointments arise which in fact need not occur. Indeed, even with comparatively adequate planning horizons, change oftentimes takes much longer than anticipated. But if given sufficient support over a long enough period, some projects that look bad and perhaps even counterproductive in the short term may look much more like successes in the longer term, as their potential constituencies slowly learn to make them effective and accountable.

It should be clear by now if it was not so at the outset of our endeavor that the union of the forestry and rural development sectors is long overdue; instead of continuing to labor in isolation, the two should be working as partners in the overall development enterprise itself. Each can profit greatly by cooperating with the other and including the other in its own efforts.

But the real benefits go far beyond such limited assistance from one sector to the other. Rural development has a long experience in failing and succeeding at just about every conceivable aspect of trying to promote change in the Third World countryside except forestry. Now that forestry has become part and parcel of the enterprise to bring positive social and economic change to the rural areas of the LDCs, it makes sense to assimilate that earlier experience and become part of it. Development professionals in both the RD and forestry sectors will improve their knowledge and effectiveness, the international donor community will be able to do a better job at the foreign aid business, academics will gain a fuller understanding of the process of promoting rural change, and finally the poor rural majority in the Third World, who do not distinguish between professional, bureaucratic or intellectual sectors as they try to secure their daily livelihoods against what are often almost insurmountable odds, are more likely to find ways to make better lives for themselves.

ABBREVIATIONS AND ACRONYMS

ADA	Adaptive development adminstration
AID	United States Agency for International Development
AMUL	Anand Milk Producers Union Limited (India)
CD	Community Development Programme(India)
CFW	Community Forestry Wing (Gujarat state, India)
CIMMYT	Centro Internacional de el Mejormiento de Maíz y Trigo
FAO	Food and Agricultural Organization of the United Nations
FSR	Farming systems research
HYV	High yielding variety
ICIHI	Independent Commission on International Humanitarian Issues
IITA	International Institute of Tropical Agriculture
IRD	Integrated rural development
IRRI	International Rice Research Institute
LDC	Less developed country
LO	Local organization
NGO	Non-governmental organization
PCPRM	Panel on Common Property Resource Management
PICOP	Paper Industries Corporation of the Philippines
PPSS	President's Private Sector Survey on Cost Control (United States)
PR	Panchayati Raj (India)
RD	Rural development
R & D	Research and development
RI	Rural institution
TVA	Tennessee Valley Authority (United States)
T &V	Traning and Visit System (World Bank)
UNICEF	United Nations Children's Fund
VFA	Village Forestry Association (South Korea)
VLW	Village level worker (India)
WRI	World Resources Institute

REFERENCES

Acharya, Meena, and Lynn Bennett (1983) *Women and the Subsistence Sector: Economic Participation and Household Decision-Making in Nepal*, World Bank Staff Working Paper #562 (Washington: World Bank).

Adams, Dale W., et. al., eds. (1984) *Undermining Rural Development with Cheap Credit* (Boulder, CO: Westview Press).

Adelman, Irma (1975) "Development Economics: A Reassessment of Goals." *American Economic Review* 65, 2 (May) *Papers and Proceedings*, 302-310.

Agarwal, Anil, and Sunita Narain, eds. (1985) *The State of India's Environment 1984-85: The Second Citizens' Report* (New Delhi: Centre for Science and Environment).

Alvares, Claude (1982) "A New Mystification?" *Development Forum* (January-February), 3-4 (Tokyo: United Nations University).

Anderson, J. N. (1982) "Rural Organizations in Law for Development: Prospects in Philippine Natural Resources Management," in International Third World Legal Studies Association, *Third World Legal Studies: 1982 -- Law in Alternative Strategies for Rural Development* (New York: International Center for Legal Studies).

Anisuzzaman, M., Badaruddin Ahmed, A. K. M. Serajul Islam and Sajjad Hussain (1986) *Comilla Models of Development: A Quarter Century of Experience* (Comilla: Bangladesh Academy for Rural Devlopment).

Aqua, Ronald (1974) *Local Institutions and Rural Development in South Korea*, Special Series on Rural Local Government (Ithaca, NY: Rural Development Committee, Center for International Studies, Cornell University).

Arnold, J. E. Michael (1983) "Replenishing the World's Forests: Community Forestry and Meeting Fuelwood Needs," *Commonwealth Forestry Review* 62, 3 (September), 183-189.

Arnold, J. E. Michael (1987) "Community Forestry," *Ambio* 16, 2-3, 122-128.

Arnold, J. E. M., and J. Gabriel Campbell (1986) "Collective Management of Hill Forests in Nepal: The Community Forestry Development Project," in PCPRM, 425-454.

Bahuguna, Sunderlal (1986) "Chipko -- The People's Movement to Protect Forests," *Cultural Survival Quarterly* 10, 3, 27-30.

Barkin, David (1972-73) "A Case Study of the Beneficiaries of Regional Development," *International Social Development Review* 4, 1-11.

Barnard, Geoffrey, and Claudio Zaror (1986) "Industry: Creator or Destroyer of Forests?" *Courier* dossier, 78-81.

Bendix, Reinhard (1969) *Nation-Building and Citizenship: Studies of Our Changing Social Order* (Garden City, NY: Anchor Books).

Benor, Daniel, James Q. Harrison and Michael Baxter (1984) *Agricultural Extension: The Training and Visit System* (Washington: World Bank).

Benor, Daniel, and Michael Baxter (1984) *Training and Visit Extension* (Washingon: World Bank).

Berry, R. Albert, and William R. Cline (1979) *Agrarian Structure and Productivity in Developing Countries* (Baltimore, MD: Johns Hopkins University Press).

Blair, Harry W. (1978) "Rural Development, Class Structure and Bureaucracy in Bangladesh," *World Development* 6:1 (January), 65-82.

Blair, Harry W. (1982) *The Political Economy of Participation in Local Development Programs: Short-term Impasse and Long-term Change in South Asia and the United States from the 1950s to the 1970s*, Monograph series No. 4 (Ithaca, NY: Rural Development Committee, Center for International Studies, Cornell University).

Blair, Harry W. (1984) "Agricultural Credit, Political Economy and Patronage," in Adams (1984: 183-193).

Blair, Harry W. (1985) "Participation, Public Policy, Political Economy and Development in Bangladesh, 1958-85," *World Development* 13, 12 (December), 1231-1247.

Blair, Harry W. (1986a) "Social Forestry in India: Time to Modify Goals?" *Economic and Political Weekly* 21, 30 (21 July), 1317-1321.

Blair, Harry W. (1986b) "Ideology, Foreign Aid and Rural Poverty in Bangladesh: Emergence of the Like-Minded Group," *Journal of Social Sciences* (Dhaka, Bangladesh) No. 34 (October), 1-27.

Blustain, Harvey (1982) "Clientelism and Local Organization," in Harvey Blustain and E. LeFranc (eds.), *Strategies for Organization of Small-Farm Agriculture in Jamaica* (Ithaca, NY: Rural Development Committee, Center for International Studies, Cornell University).

Bogach, V. Susan (1985) *Wood as Fuel: Energy for Developing Countries* (New York: Praeger).

Bonkoungo, E., and R. Catino (1986) "Wood, Land, People," *Courier* dossier, 82-84.

Boserup, Ester (1970) *Woman's Role in Economic Development* (New York: St. Martin's Press).

Boserup, Ester, and Christine Lijencrantz (1975) *Integration of Women in Development: Why, When, How* (New York: United Nations Development Programme).

Braibanti, Ralph, ed. (1969) *Political and Administrative Development* (Durham: Duke University Press).

Brammer, Hugh (1980) "Some Innovations Don't Wait for Experts: A Report on Applied Research by Bangladesh Peasants," *Ceres* 13 (March-April), 24-28.

Brechin, Steven R., and Patrick C. West (1982) "Social Barriers in Implementing Appropriate Technology : The Case of Community Forestry in Niger, West Africa," *Humboldt Journal of Social Relations* 9, 2 (Spring/Summer), 81-94.

Brown, Lester R. (1970) *Seeds of Change: The Green Revolution and Development in the 1970s* (New York: Praeger).

Bryant, Coralie, and Louise G. White (1982) *Managing Development in the Third World* (Boulder, CO: Westview Press).

Buchanan, James M. (1977) "Why Does Government Grow?" in Thomas E. Borcherding, ed., *Budget and Bureaucrats: The Sources of Government Growth* (Durham, NC: Duke University Press).

Buttel, F. H., and W. L. Flinn (1974) "The Structure of Support for the Environmental Movement, 1968-1970," *Rural Sociology* 39, 1, 56-69.

Byerlee, Derek, Larry Harrington and Donald L. Winkelman (1982) "Farming Systems Research: Issues in Research Strategy and Technology Design," *American Journal of Agricultural Economics* 64, 5 (December), 897-904.

Cassen, Robert (1975) "Welfare and Population: Notes on Rural India Since 1950," *Population and Development Review* 1:1 (September), 33-70.

Caudill, Harry M. (1963) *Night Comes to the Cumberlands* (Boston: Little Brown).

Cerescope (1983)"'Poor Man's Meat,' Pulses Lose Ground to Cereal Expansion," *Ceres* 16:3 (May-June), 10-12.

Cernea, Michael (1981) *Land Tenure Systems and Social Implications of Forestry Development Programs.* Staff Working Paper No. 452 (Washington: World Bank).

Cernea, Michael M., John K. Coulter and John F. A. Russell, eds. (1985) *Research-Extension-Farmer: A Two-Way Continuum for Agricultural Development* (Washington: World Bank).

Chambers, Robert (1983) *Rural Development: Putting the Last First* (London: Longman).

Chambers, Robert (1986) "Normal Professionalism, New Paradigms and Development," Discussion Paper 227 ((Brighton: Institute of Development Studies, University of Sussex).

Chambers, Robert, and Janice Jiggins (1987) "Agricultural Research for Resource-Poor Farmers -- Part I: Transfer-of-Technology and Farming Systems Research," and "Part II: A Parsimonious Paradigm," *Agricultural Administration and Extension* 27, 1, 35-52 and 27, 2, 109-128.

Chambers, Robert, and Robert Wade (1980) "Managing the Main System: Irrigation's Blind Spot," *Economic and Political Weekly* 15 (27 September), A107-A112.

Chandrashekar, D. M., B. V. Krishna Murthi and S. R. Ramaswamy (1987) "Social Forestry in Karnataka: An Impact Analysis," *Economic and Political Weekly* 22, 24 (13 June), 935-941.

Cheema, G. Shabbir, and Dennis A. Rondinelli, eds. (1983) *Decentralization and Development: Policy Implementation in Developing Countries* (Beverly Hills, CA: Sage Publications).

Chenery, Hollis, et. al. (1974) *Redistribution with Growth* (London: Oxford University Press).

Chenery, Hollis (1975)"The Structuralist Approach to Development Policy," *American Economic Review* 65, 2 (May) *Papers and Proceedings*, 310-400.

Chenery, Hollis (1979) *Structural Change and Development Policy* (New York: Oxford University Press).

Chuta, Enyima, and Carl Liedholm (1979) *Rural Non-Farm Employment: A Review of the State of the Art*, MSU Rural Development Paper #4.

(East Lansing: Michigan State University, Department of Agricultural Economics).

Claiborne, William (1984) "Indian Peasants Hope Tree Farming Will Make Them Rich," *Washington Post* (22 April).

Cohen, John and Norman Uphoff (1977) *Rural Development Participation: Concepts and Measures for Project Design, Implementation and Evaluation.* (Ithaca, NY: Rural Development Committee, Cornell University).

Commander, Simon (1986) "Managing Indian Forests: A Case for the Reform of Property Rights," Social Forestry Network Paper 3b (London: ODI Agricultural Administration Unit).

Conyers, Diana (1981) "Papua New Guinea: Decentralization and Development from the Middle," in Walter B. Stöhr and D. R. Fraser Taylor, eds., *Development from Above or Below?* (Chichester: John Wiley & Sons), 209-229.

Conyers, Diana (1982) *Decentralization for Development: A Select Annotated Bibliography* (London: Commonwealth Secretariat).

Conyers, Diana (1984a) "Decentralization and Development: A Review of the Literature," *Public Administration and Development* 4, 2 (April-June), 187-197.

Conyers, Diana (1984b) "Decentralization: The Latest Fashion in Development Administration?" *Public Administration and Development* 3, 2 (April-June), 97-109.

Conyers, Diana (1986) "Future Directions in Development Studies: The Case of Decentralization," *World Development* 14, 5 (May), 593-603.

Coombs, Philip H., ed. (1980) *Meeting the Needs of the Rural Poor: The Integrated Community-Based Approach* (New York: Pergamon Press).

Cordell, John C., and Margaret A. McKean (1986) "Sea Tenure in Bahia, Brazil," in PCPRM, 85-114.

Courier dossier (Gerald Foley et al.) (1986) "The Woodfuel Crisis: Towards a New Understanding," *Courier* (European Economic Community) No. 95 (January-February). This "dossier" contains a number of individual articles on woodfuel issues.

Crook, Isabel, and David Crook (1979) *Ten Mile Inn: Mass Movement in a Chinese Village* (New York: Pantheon Books).

Davidson, Andrew P. (1987) "Does Farming Systems Research Have a Future?" *Agricultural Administration and Extension* 24, 2, 69-77.

Day, Jennie (1981) "Gambian Women: Unequal Partners in Rice Development Projects," *The Journal of Development Studies* 17, 3 (April).

Denning, Glenn L. (1985) "Integrating Agricultural Extension Programs with Farming Systems Research," in Cernea et al. (1985: 113-135).

Dorner, Peter (1972) *Land Reform and Economic Development* (Harmondsworth: Penguin Books).

Dorner, Peter, and Rodolfo Quiros (1973) "Institutional Dualism in Central America's Agricultural Development," *Journal of Latin American Studies*, 5:2 (November), 217-32.

Douglin, David, Peter Doan and Norman Uphoff (1984) *Local Institutional Development for Natural Resource Management*, Special Series on Local Institutional Development No. 2 (Ithaca, NY: Cornell University, Center for International Studies, Rural Development Committee).

Dumont, René, and Nicholas Cohen (1980) *The Growth of Hunger: A New Politics of Agriculture* (London: Marion Boyars).

Durham, William H. (1979) *Scarcity and Survival in Central America: Ecological Origins of the Soccer War* (Stanford: Stanford University Press).

Eckholm, Erik (1979) *Planting for the Future: Forestry for Human Needs*, Worldwatch Paper No. 26 (Washington: Worldwatch Institute).

Esman, Milton J. and Norman Uphoff (1982) *Local Organization and Rural Development: The State-of-the-Art.* Ithaca, NY: Rural Development Committee, Center for International Relations, Cornell University.

Esman, Milton J., and Norman Uphoff (1984) *Local Organizations: Intermediaries in Rural Development.* (Ithaca, NY: Cornell University Press).

FAO (Food and Agricultural Organization of the United Nations) (1981) *Republic of Korea Forestry for Local Community Development: Report on a Study Tour.* Forestry for Local Community Development Programme, GCP/INT/347/SWE (Rome: FAO).

FAO (1985a) *Tree Growing by Rural People.* FAO Forestry Paper 64 (Rome: FAO).

FAO (1985b) *Evaluation of the Gujarat Social Forestry Programme: Final Report to the Government of India,* GCP/INT/363/SWE-India (Rome: FAO).

FAO (1985c) *The Ecological Effects of Eucalyptus.* FAO Forestry Paper 59 (Rome: FAO).

Feder, Gershon, and Roger Slade (1984) "Aspects of the Training and Visit System of Agricultural Extension in India: A Comparative Analysis," Staff Working Paper No. 656 (Washington: World Bank).

Foley, Gerald (1986) "Woodfuel: The Energy Crisis of the Poor," *Courier* dossier, 66-69.

Foley, Gerald, and Geoffrey Barnard (1984) *Farm and Community Forestry.* Energy Information Programme, Technical Report No. 3 (London: Earthscan -- International Institute for Environment and Development).

Fortmann, Louise (1980) *Peasants, Officials and Participation in Rural Tanzania: Experience with Villagization and Decentralization,* RLO No. 1 (Ithaca, NY: Cornell University, Center for International Studies, Rural Development Committee).

Fortmann, Louise, and James Riddell (1985) *Trees and Tenure: An Annotated Bibliography for Agroforestrers and Others* (Madison: Land Tenure Center, University of Wisconsin; and Nairobi: International Council for Research in Agroforestry).

Fortmann, Louise, and Dianne Rocheleau (1984) "Why Agroforestry Needs Women: Four Myths and a Case Study," *Unasylva* 36, 4 (No. 146), 2-12.

Fortmann, Louise, and Emery Roe (1981) *The Water Points Survey* (Gaborone, Botswana: Ministry of Agriculture).

Foucault, Michel (1977) *Discipline and Punish: The Birth of the Prison* (New York: Pantheon Books).

Franke, Richard W., and Barbara H. Chasin (1980) *Seeds of Famine: Ecological Destruction and the Development Dilemma in the West African Sahel* (Montclair, NJ: Allanheld, Osmun).

Fraser, Arvonne (1977) *Women in Development* (Washington: Agency for International Development).

Freeman, Peter H., and Tim Resch (1985/6) "Large Plantations of Rapidly Growing Exotic Species: Lessons from the Bandia, Senegal," *Rural Africana* 23-24 (Fall-Winter), 87-93.

George, Susan (1977) *How the Other Half Dies: The Real Reasons for World Hunger* (Montclair, NJ: Allanheld, Osmun).

Germaine, Adrienne (1976-77) "Poor Rural Women: A Policy Perspective," *Journal of International Affairs*, 30, 2 (Fall/Winter), 161-172.

Gerth, H. H., and C. Wright Mills, eds. (1958) *From Max Weber: Essays in Sociology* (New York: Oxford University Press).

Gettens, John (1982) "Amul: Factors Influencing Success," unpublished manuscript (Ithaca, NY: Government Department, Cornell University [December]).

Gibbs, Christopher (1982) "Institutional Obstacles to Effective Forestry for Local Community Development in Asia," paper for USAID Conference on Forestry and Development in Asia, Bangalore, India,

Conference on Forestry and Development in Asia, Bangalore, India, 19-23 April.

Gilbert, Elon H., David W. Norman and Fred E. Winch (1980) *Farming Systems Research: A Critical Appraisal*, MSU Rural Development Paper No. 6 (East Lansing: Michigan State University, Department of Agricultural Economics).

Goldsmith, Arthur A., and Harvey S. Blustain (1980) *Local Organizations and Participation in Integrated Rural Development in Jamaica*, RLO No. 3 (Ithaca, NY: Cornell University, Center for International Studies, Rural Development Committee).

Golembiewski, Robert T. (1977a) "A Critique of 'Democratic Administration' and its Supporting Ideation," *American Political Science Review* 71, 4 (December), 1488-1507.

Golembiewski, Robert T. (1977b) "Observations on 'Doing Political Theory': A Rejoinder," *American Political Science Review* 71, 4 (December), 1526-1531.

Gotsch, Carl H. (1973) "Tractor Mechanization and Rural Development in Pakistan," *International Labour Review*, 107, 2 (February), 133-66.

Goulet, Denis (1971) *The Cruel Choice: A New Concept in the Theory of Development*. (New York: Atheneum).

Government of India (1980) Planning Commission, Programme Evaluation Organization, *Joint Evaluation Report on Employment Guarantee Scheme of Maharashtra (April 1976 - October 1978)*, (Delhi: Controller of Publications).

Government of Pakistan (1980) *Pakistan Economic Survey, 1979-80* (Islamabad: Government of Pakistan, Finance Division, Economic Adviser's Wing).

Gran, Guy (1983) *Development by People: Citizen Construction of a Just World* (New York: Praeger).

Grant, James P. (1973) "Development: An End of the Trickle Down?" *Foreign Policy* 12 (Fall), 43-65.

Gray, Cheryl Williamson (1982) *Food Consumption Parameters for Brazil and Their Application to Food Policy*, Research Report 32 (Washington: International Food Policy Research Institute).

Greeley, Martin (1982) "Rural Technology, Rural Insitutions and the Rural Poorest: The Case of Rice Processing in Bangladesh," in Martin Greeley and Michael Howes, eds., *Rural Technology, Rural Institutions and the Rural Poorest* (Comilla, Bangladesh: Center on Integrated Rural Development for Asia and the Pacific), 128-151.

Gregersen, H. M. (1982) *Village Forestry Development in the Republic of Korea: A Case Study*. Forestry for Local Community Development Programme, GCP/INT/347/SWE (Rome: FAO).

Griffin, Keith (1974) *The Political Economy of Agrarian Change: An Essay on the Green Revolution* (Cambridge: Harvard University Press).

Guha, Ramachandra (1985) "Scientific Forestry and Social Change in Uttarakhand," *Economic and Political Weekly* 20, 45-47 (November Special Number), 1939-1952.

Hageboeck, Molly, and Mary Beth Allen (1982) "Private Sector: Ideas and Opportunities, A Review of Basic Concepts and Selected Experiences," AID Program Evaluation Discussion Paper No. 14 (Washington: Agency for International Development, Bureau for Program and Policy Coordination, Office of Evaluation).

Hanke, Steve H. (1983) "Land Policy," in Holwill (1983: 181-191).

Haragopal, G. (1980) *Administrative Leadership and Rural Development in India* (New Delhi: Light and Life Publishers).

Hardin, Garrett (1968) "The Tragedy of the Commons," *Science* 162 (13 December), 1243-1248.

Hartfiel, Ann (1982) "Two Women's Production Cooperatives," *Grassroots Development*, 6, 1 (Washington: Inter-American Foundation).

Heermans, John G. (1985/6) "The Guesselbodi Experiment: Bushland Management in Niger," *Rural Africana* 23-24 (Fall-Winter), 67-77.

Helleine, G. K. (1975) "The Role of the Multinational Corporations in the Less Developed Countries' Trade and Technology," *World Development* 3, 4 (April), 161-189.

Hinton, William (1968) *Fanshen: A Documentary of Revolution in a Chinese Village* (New York: Random House Vintage Books).

Hirschman, Albert O. (1958) *The Strategy of Economic Development* (New Haven: Yale University Press).

Holwill, Richard H., ed. (1983) *Agenda '83: A Mandate for Leadership Report* (Washington: Heritage Foundation)

Hoskins, Marilyn W. (1979) *Women in Forestry for Local Community Development: A Programming Guide*. Report No. AID-OTR-147-79-83 (Washington: US Agency for International Development).

Hoskins, Marilyn W. (1982) "Social Forestry in West Africa: Myths and Realities," paper presented at American Association for the Advancement of Science annual meeting, Washington.

Hoskins, Marilyn W. (1983) "Mobilizing Rural Communities," *Unasylva* 35, No. 142, 12-13.

Hyden, Goren (1983) *No Shortcuts to Progress: African Development Management in Perspective* (London: Heinemann).

Hyman, Eric L. (1983) "Pulpwood Treefarming in the Philippines from the Viewpoint of the Smallholder: An Ex Post Evaluation of the PICOP Project," *Agricultural Administration* 14, 1, 23-49.

ICIHI (Independent Commission on International Humanitarian Issues) (1986) *The Encroaching Desert: The Consequences of Human Failure* (London: Zed Books).

Ickis, John C., Edilberto de Jesus and Rushikesh Maru, eds. (1987) *Beyond Bureaucracy: Strategic Management of Social Development* (West Hartford, CT: Kumarian Press).

Jain, Shobita (1984) "Standing up for Trees: Women's Role in the Chipko Movement," *Unasylva* 36, 4 (No. 146), 12-20.

Java, Ramesh (1986) "Project Completion Report: Gujarat Community Forest Project, Phase-I" (Vadodara, India: Gjuarat State Forestry Department).

Johl, S.S., and Mohinder S. Mudahar (1974) *The Dynamics of Institutional Change and Rural Development in Punjab, India*, Special Series on Rural Local Government (Ithaca, NY: Rural Development Committee, Center for International Studies, Cornell University).

Johnson, Ronald N., and John Baden (1983) "A Positive Sum Timber Harvest Policy," in Holwill (1983: 41-47).

Johnstone, Bruce F. and Peter Kilby (1975) *Agriculture and Structural Transformation: Economic Strategies in Late Developing Countries*, (New York: Oxford University Press).

Karamchandani, Kanayo P. (1982) "Gujarat Social Forestry Program: A Case Study," draft mimeo. (Vadodara: Gujarat Forestry Department).

Kennedy, James (1985) "Conceiving Forest Management as Providing for Current and Future Social Value," *Forest Ecology and Management* 13, 1/2 (November), 121-132.

Khan, Asmeen (1986) "A Hundred Recent Journal Articles on Social Forestry," Social Forestry Network Paper 2e (London: ODI Agricultural Administration Unit).

Kilby, P. (1982) "Small-Scale Industry in Kenya," MSU Department of Agricultural Economics, Working Paper #20 (East Lansing: Michigan State University).

Kneerim, Jill (1980) *Village Women Organize: The Mraru Bus Service*, Seeds Pamphlet Series, Population Council, Carnegie Corporation and the Ford Foundation.

Knight, Peter T., Dennis Mahar and Ricardo Moran (1979) Annex III: "Health, Nutrition and Education," in Peter T. Knight et. al., *Brazil: Human Resources Special Report* (Washington: World Bank, 1979).

Korten, David C. (1980) "Community Organization and Rural Development: A Learning Process Approach," *Public Administration Review* 40: 5 (September-October), 480-511.

Korten, David C., ed. (1987) *Community Management: Asian Experience and Perspective* (West Hartford, CT: Kumarian Press).

Korten, David C., and Felipe B. Alfonso, eds. (1983) *Bureaucracy and the Poor: Closing the Gap* (West Hartford, CT: Kumarian Press).

Korten, David C., and Rudi Klauss, eds. (1984) *People Centered Development: Contributions Toward Theory and Planning Frameworks* (West Hartford, CT: Kumarian Press).

Korten, David C., and Norman T. Uphoff (1981) *Bureaucratic Reorientation for Participatory Rural Development*, NASPAA Working paper No. 1 (Washington: National Association of Schools of Public Affairs and Administration).

Kronick, J. (1984) "Temporal Analysis of Agroforestry Systems for Rural Development," *Agroforestry Systems* 2, 3, 165-176.

Laarman, Jan G. (1986) "A Perspective on Private Enterprise and Development Aid for Forestry," *Commonwealth Forestry Review* 65, 4 (December), 315-320.

LaPalombara, Joseph, ed. (1963) *Bureaucracy and Political Development* (Princeton, NJ: Princeton University Press).

Lipton, Michael (1977) *Why Poor People Stay Poor: Urban Bias in World Development* (London: Temple Smith).

Maddock, Nicholas (1987) "Privatizing Agriculture: Policy Options in Developing Countries," *Food Policy* 12, 4 (November), 295-298.

Mahiti Team (1983) "A Question: Why Is Social Forestry Not Social?", paper prepared for Ford Foundation Workshop on Social Forestry and Voluntary Agencies, Bradhkal Lake, Haryana, India, 13-15 April, mimeo (Dhanduka Taluka, Ahmedabad District, Gujarat: Mahiti Team).

Marcotte, Paul, and Louis E. Swanson (1987) "The Disarticulation of Farming Systems Research with National Agricultural Systems: Bringing FSR Back In," *Agricultural Administration and Extension* 27, 2, 75-91.

Mayer, Albert, et al. (1958) *Pilot Project India: The Story of Rural Development at Etawah, Uttar Pradesh* (Berkeley: University of California Press).

Mazumdar, Vina (n.d.) "Traditional Women and Their Integration into Modern Development: An Emerging into Two Models in India," unpublished manuscript (New Delhi: Indian Council of Social Science Research).

Mellor, John W. (1966) *The Economics of Agricultural Development* (Ithaca, NY: Cornell University Press).

Mellor, John W. (1976) *The New Economics of Growth: A Strategy for India and the Developing World* (Ithaca, NY: Cornell University Press).

Mnzava, E. M. (1982) *Village Afforestation: Lessons of Experience in Tanzania*, TF/INT 271 (SWE) (Rome: FAO Forestry Department).

Montagne, Pierre (1985/6) "Contributions of Indigenous Silviculture to Forestry Development in Rural Areas: Examples from Niger and Mali," *Rural Africana* 23-24 (Fall-Winter), 61-65.

Moore, Mick (1984) "Institutional Development, the World Bank, and India's New Agricultural Extension Programme," *Journal of Development Studies* 20, 4 (July), 313-317.

Morris, Morris D. (1980) "The Physical Quality of Life Index," *Development Digest* 18(1), 95-100.

Morss, Elliot R., J. K. Hatch, D. R. Mickelwait, and C. F. Sweet (1976) *Strategies for Small Farmer Development* (Boulder, CO: Westview Press).

Murdoch, William W. (1980) *The Poverty of Nations: The Political Economy of Hunger and Population* (Baltimore: Johns Hopkins University Press).

Myrdal, Gunnar (1957) *Rich Lands and Poor* (New York: Harper).

Myrdal, Gunnar (1968) *Asian Drama: An Enquiry into the Poverty of Nations* (New York: Pantheon).

Nicholson, Norman K., and Dilawar Ali Khan (1974) *Local Institutions and Rural Development in Pakistan*, RLG Monograph No. 10 (Ithaca, NY: Cornell University, Center for International Studies, Rural Development Comittee).

Norgaard, Richard B. (1984) "Traditional Agricultural Knowledge: Past Performance, Future Prospects and Institutional Implications," *American Journal of Agricultural Economics* 66,5 (December), 874-878.

O'Keefe, Phil, Calestous Juma and Jean-Marion Aitken (1986) "Wood in Towns: No Money to Burn," *Courier* dossier, 74-77.

Okonjo, Ramene (1979) "Rural Womens' Credit Systems: A Nigerian Example," *Learning About Rural Women*, Sondra Zeidenstein (ed.), *Studies in Family Planning* (New York: Population Council) 10, 11-12, 309-422.

Olpadwala, Porus D. (1985) "Appropriate Technology for Forest Industries," paper prepared for FAO Forestry Department, Rome.

Ostrom, Elinor (1986) "Issues of Definition and Theory: Some Conclusions and Hypotheses," in PCPRM, 597-614.

Ostrom, Vincent (1977) "Some Problems in Doing Political Theory: A Response to Golembiewski's 'Critique'," *American Political Science Review* 71, 4 (December), 1508-1525.

Ostrom, Vincent, and Elinor Ostrom (1977) "Public Goods and Public Choices," in E. S. Savas, ed., *Alternatives for Delivering Public Services: Toward Improved Performance* (Boulder, CO: Westview Press), 7-49.

Owens, Edgar F., and Robert Shaw (1972) *Development Reconsidered: Bridging the Gap Between Government and People* (Lexington, MA: Lexington Books).

Pastore, J. (1977) "Brazilian Agricultural Research: Export vs. Nutrition," *Food Policy* 2,3 (August), 217-27.

Patel, Surendra J. (1979) "Trademarks and the Third World," *World Development* 7, 7 (July), 653-662.

Paul, Samuel (1982) *Managing Development Programs: The Lessons of Success* (Boulder, CO: Westview Press).

PCPRM (Panel on Common Property Resource Management) (1986) *Proceedings of the Conference on Common Property Resource Management*, Board of Science and Technology for International Development (Washington: National Academy Press).

PPSS (President's Private Sector Survey on Cost Control) (1983a) *Report on the Department of the Interior* (Washington: Government Printing Office).

PPSS (1983b) *Report on the Department of Agriculture* (Washington: Government Printing Office).

Prosterman, Roy L., and Jeffrey M. Reidigger (1987) *Land Reform and Democractic Development* (Baltimore: Johns Hopkins).

Raintree, John B., ed. (1987) *Land, Trees and Tenure: Proceedings of an International Workshop on Tenure Issues in Agroforestry, Nairobi, May 27-31, 1985* (Nairobi: International Council for Research in Agroforestry; and Madison: Land Tenure Center, University of Wisconsin).

Raphaeli, Nimrod, ed. (1967) *Readings in Comparative Public Administration* (Boston: Allyn and Bacon).

Raulet, Harry M. (1976) "The Historical Context of Pakistan's Rural Economy," in Stevens et. al. (1976: 198-213).

Reynolds, Norman, and Pushpa Sundar (1977) "Maharashtra's Employment Guarantee Scheme: A Programme to Emulate?" *Economic and Political Weekly* 12:29 (July 16), 1149-58.

Robock, Stefan H. (1966) "Strategies for Regional Economic Development," *Papers of the Regional Science Association*, 17, 129-141.

Romm, Jeff (1986) "Forest Policy and Development Policy," *Journal of World Forest Resource Management* 2, 2, 85-103.

Rondinelli, Dennis A. (1983) *Development Projects as Policy Experiments: An Adaptive Approach to Development Administration* (London: Methuen).

Rondinelli, Dennis A. (1987) *Development Administration and U. S. Foreign Policy* (Boulder, CO: Lynne Rienner Publishers).

Rostow, W. W. (1960) *The Stages of Economic Growth: A Non-Communist Manifesto* (Cambridge: Cambridge University Press).

Roth, Gabriel (1987) *The Private Provision of Public Services in Developing Countries* (New York: Oxford University Press).

Russell, Clifford S., and Norman K. Nicholson, eds. (1981) *Public Choice and Rural Development*. Research Paper R-21 (Washington: Resources for the Future).

Saint, William S., and E. Walter Coward, Jr. (1977) "Agriculture and Behavioral Science: Emerging Orientations," *Science* 197, No. 4305 (19 August), 733-37.

Savas, E. S. (1987) *Privatization: The Key to Better Government* (Chatham, NJ: Chatham House Publishers).

Schaffer, Bernard (1977) *Official Providers: Access, Equity and Participation* (Paris: UNESCO, Division for the Study of Development).

Schaffer, Bernard, and Geoff Lamb (1981) *Can Equity Be Organized? Equity, Development Analysis and Planning* (Farnborough, UK: Gower).

Scott, James C. (1972) *Comparative Political Corruption* (Englewood Cliffs, NJ: Prentice-Hall).

Scott, James C. (1985) *Weapons of the Weak: Everyday Forms of Peasant Resistance* (New Haven: Yale University Press).

Seers, Dudley (1969) "The Meaning of Development," *International Development Review* 11, 4 (December), 2-6.

Shah, Tushaar (1987) "Gains from Social Forestry: Lessons from West Bengal," Network Paper No. 5e (London: ODI Agricultural Administration, Social Forestry Network).

Shiva, Vandana, and J. Bandyopadhyay (1986) "The Evolution, Structure and Impact of the Chipko Movement," *Mountain Research and Development* 6, 2 (May), 133-142.

Shiva, Vandana, H. C. Sharatchandra and J. Bandyopadhyay (1982) "Social Forestry -- No Solution Within the Market Place," *Ecologist* 12, 4 (September), 158-168.

Shiva, Vandana, H. C. Sharatchandra and J. Bandyopadhyay (1987) "Social Forestry for Whom?" in Korten (1987), 238-246.

Sinha, Radha (1976) *Food & Poverty* (London: Crown Helm).

Skutsch, M. M. (1985) "Dissemination of Energy Technologies: Stove and Forestry Projects in Gujarat," in W. Palz, J. Coombs and D. O. Hall, eds., *Energy from Biomass, 3rd E. C. Conference* (London: Elsevier Applied Science).

Smith, B. C. (1985) *Decentralization: The Territorial Dimension of the State* (London: George Allen & Unwin).

Smith, Brian C. (1986) "Spatial Ambiguities: Decentralization within the State," *Public Administration and Development* 6, 4 (October-December), 455-465.

Somjee, A. H. and Geeta Somjee (1978) "Cooperative Dairying and the Profiles of Social Change in India," *Economic Development and Cultural Change* 26, 3 (April), 577-590.

Spitz, Pierre (1978) "Silent Violence: Famine and Inequality," *International Social Science Journal* 30, 4, 867-892.

Stavis, Benedict (1974) *Rural Local Governance and Agricultural Development in Taiwan*, Special Series on Rural Local Government (Ithaca, NY: Rural Development Committee, Center for International Studies, Cornell University).

Stevens, Robert D., Hamza Alavi and Peter J. Bertocci, eds. (1976) *Rural Development in Bangladesh and Pakistan* (Honolulu: University Press of Hawaii).

Stewart, Frances (1977) *Technology and Underdevelopment* (Boulder, CO: Westview Press).

Streeten, Paul P. (1980) "Basic Needs and Human Rights," *World Development* 8, 2 (February), 107-111.

Tai, Hung-chao (1974) *Land Reform and Politics: A Comparative Analysis* (Berkeley: University of California Press).

Thai Khandi Research Institute (1980) *A Self-Help Organization in Rural Thailand: The Question of Appropriate Inputs* (Bangkok: Thammesat University).

Thomas, Elizabeth Marshall (1958) *The Harmless People* (New York: Random House, Vintage Books).

Thomas, John Woodward, and Richard M. Hook (1977) *Creating Rural Employment: A Manual for Organizing Rural Works Programs* (Washington: U.S. Agency for International Development).

Thomson, James T. (1981) "Public Choice Analysis of Institutional Constraints on Firewood Production Strategies in the West African Sahel," in Russel and Nicholson (1981: 119-152).

Thomson, James T., David H. Feeny and Ronald J. Oakerson (1986) "Institutional Dynamics: The Evolution and Dissolution of Common Property Resource Management," in PCPRM, 391-424.

Thompson, E. P. (1967) "Time, Work, Discipline and Industrial Capitalism," *Past and Present* 38 (December, 56-97).

Thrupp, L. A. (1984) "Women, Wood and Work: In Kenya and Beyond," *Unasylva* 36, No. 146, 36-43.

Turnbull, Colin M. (1962) *The Forest People* (New York: Simon and Schuster).

Uphoff, Norman (1982-83) "The Institutional-Organizer (IO) Programme in the Field after Ten Months: A Report on Trip to Ampare/Gal Oya, Sri Lanka, January 14-17, 1982." Similar reports update the project after sixteen and twenty-seven months. (Ithaca, NY: Center for International Studies, Cornell University).

Uphoff, Norman T. (1986a) *Improving International Irrigation Management with Farmer Participation: Getting the Process Right* (Boulder, CO: Westview Press).

Uphoff, Norman T. (1986b) *Local Institutional Development: An Analytical Casebook with Cases* (West Hartford, CT: Kumarian Press).

Uphoff, Norman T. (1987) "Activating Community Capacity for Water Management in Sri Lanka," in Korten (1987), 201-219.

Uphoff, Norman, John Cohen and William Goldsmith (1979) Feasibility and Application of Participation: A State-of-the-Art Paper. Ithaca, NY: Rural Development Committee, Center for International Studies, Cornell University.

USAID (United States Agency for International Development) (1982) "A.I.D. Policy Paper: Private Enterprise Development," mimeo. (Washington: USAID, Bureau for Program and Policy Coordination).

USAID (1987) "Decentralization: Finance and Management," Project Paper 936-5446 (Washington: USAID, Science and Technology Bureau, Office of Rural Development).

Vaitsos, C. (1979) "Government Policies for Bargaining with Transnational Enterprises in the Acquisition of Technology," in Jairam Ramesh and Charles Wein, Jr., *Mobilizing Technology for World Development* (New York: Praeger).

Visaria, Pravin (1982) *Size of Holding, Living Standards and Employment in Rural Western India 1972-73*, World Bank Staff Working Paper No. 459 (Washington: World Bank).

Wade, Robert (1982) "The System of Administrative and Political Corruption: Canal Irrigation in South India," *Journal of Development Studies* 18, 3 (April), 287-328.

Wade, Robert (1986) "Common Property Resource Management in South Indian Villages," in PCPRM, 231-258.

Wade, Robert (1987) "The Management of Common Property Resources: Finding a Cooperative Solution," *World Bank Research Observer* 2, 2 (July), 219-234.

Walsh, M. W. (1985) "Mixed Blessing: Sorghum Creates Joy and Trouble in Mexico as Corn is Supplemented," *Wall Street Journal*, 31 July.

Wasserstrom, Robert (1982) "La Liberatad: A Women's Cooperative in Highland Bolivia," *Grassroots Development* 6,1, 7-12 (Washington: Inter-American Foundation).

Wells, Louis T. (1973) "Economic Man and Engineering Man: Choice in a Low Wage Country," *Public Policy* 21, 3 (Summer) 319-342.

White, Louise G. (1987) *Creating Opportunities for Change: Approaches to Managing Development Programs* (Boulder, CO: Lynne Reiner Publishers).

Wiff, Mercedes (1984) "Honduras: Women Make a Start in Agroforestry," *Unasylva* 36, 4 (No. 146), 21-26.

Williams, Robert G. (1986) *Export Agriculture and the Crisis in Central America* (Chapel Hill: University of North Carolina Press).

Wood, Geoffrey D. (1980) "How the Interests of the Rural Poor Can Be Included in the Second Five-Year Plan" (Dacca: Ministry of Agriculture and Forests, Government of Bangladesh, mimeo).

Wood, Geoffrey D. (1982) *The Socialisation of Minor Irrigation in Bangladesh* (Dhaka: PROSHIKA).

World Bank (1976) *Village Water Supply: A World Bank Paper* (Washington: World Bank).

World Bank (1978) *Rural Enterprise and Non-Farm Development* (Washington: World Bank).

World Bank (1981) *Economic Development and the Private Sector* (a series of reprints from Finance and Development) (Washington: World Bank).

World Bank (1983) *World Development Report 1983* (Washington: World Bank).

World Bank (1985) *Agricultural Research and Extension: An Evaluation of the World Bank's Experience* (Washington: World Bank).

WRI (World Resources Institute) (1985) *Tropical Forests: A Call for Action* (Washington: World Resources Institute).

INDEX OF NAMES

Acharya, Meena, 129, 175
Adams, Dale W., 26, 175
Adelman, Irma, 49, 175
Agarwal, Anil, 8, 12n, 163, 175
Ahmed, Badaruddin, 175
Aitken, Jean-Marion, 190
Alavi, Hamza, 194
Alfonso, Felipe B., 111n, 188
Allen, Mary Beth, 101, 185
Alvares, Claude, 163, 175
Anderson, J. N., 79, 175
Anisuzzaman, M., 140, 175
Aqua, Ronald, 19, 176
Arnold, J. E. Michael, xii, 17, 30, 35, 86, 103, 176
Ayub Khan, M., 106, 139
Baden, John, 101, 187
Bahuguna, Sunderlal, 85, 176
Bandyopadhyay, J., 85, 193
Barkin, David, 126, 176
Barnard, Geoffrey, 5, 12n, 17, 42, 47, 64, 123, 133, 176, 182
Baxter, Michael, 110, 176
Bendix, Reinhard, 43, 176
Bennett, Lynn, 175
Benor, Daniel, 110, 176
Berry, R. Albert, 53n, 176
Bertocci, Peter J., 194
Bhatty, Zarina, xii
Blair, Harry W., xi, xii, 19, 26, 59, 86, 101, 102, 112n, 130, 136n, 156n, 176, 177
Blustain, Harvey, 80, 83, 108, 177, 184
Bogach, V. Susan, 30, 177
Bonkoungo, E., 86, 177
Boserup, Ester, 128, 129, 177
Braibanti, Ralph, 35n, 177
Brammer, Hugh, 34, 178

Brechin, Steven R., 27, 30, 63, 94, 178
Brokensha, David, 34
Brown, Lester R., 45, 178
Bryant, Coralie, 35n, 108, 178
Buchanan, James M., 111n, 178
Burch, William, xii
Burford, Anne, 101
Buttel, F. H., 29, 178
Byerlee, Derek, 113n, 178
Campbell, Gabriel, 30, 86, 103, 176
Cassen, Robert, 37, 178
Catino, R., 86, 177
Caudill, Harry M., 125, 178
Cernea, Michael M., 63, 110, 113n, 179
Chambers, Robert, 24, 27, 28, 33, 34, 93, 94, 110, 179
Chandrasekharan, C., xii
Chandrashekhar, D. M., 163, 167n, 179
Chasin, Barbara H., 38, 161, 183
Cheema, G. Shabbir, 112n, 179
Chenery, Hollis, 45, 49, 179, 180
Chetwynd, Eric, xii
Chipeta, Mafa, xii
Chuta, Enyima, 122, 180
Claiborne, William, 12n, 180
Cline, William R., 53n, 176
Cohen, John, 49, 82, 87n, 180, 196
Cohen, Nicholas, 112n, 181
Commander, Simon, 30, 107, 180
Connerly, Edwin, xii, 112n
Conyers, Diana, xii, 107, 112n, 180
Coombs, Philip H., 113n, 181

Cordell, John C., 102, 181
Coulter, John K., 179
Coward, E. Walter, 160, 193
Crook, Isabel, 65n, 181
Crook, David, 65n, 181
Davidson, Andrew P., 108, 181
Day, Jennie, 130, 181
de Jesus, Edilberto, 187
Denning, Glenn L., 110, 181
Doan, Peter, 181
Dorner, Peter, 53n, 161, 181
Douglin, David, 112n, 181
Dumont, René, 112n, 181
Durham, William H., 161, 182
Eckholm, Erik, 12n, 85, 182
Esman, Milton J., xi, 74, 84, 87n, 182
Feder, Gershon, 110, 182
Feeny, David H., 195
Finen, Gerald, xii
Fisher, Harold, xii
Flinn, W. L., 29, 178
Foley, Gerald, 5, 12n, 17, 35, 42, 47, 64, 130, 133, 182
Fortmann, Louise, xii, 23, 62, 83, 131, 150, 156n, 169, 183
Foucault, Michel, 93, 183
Franke, Richard W., 38, 161, 183
Fraser, Arvonne, 128, 183
Freeman, Peter H., 30, 183
Gandhi, Indira, 147
Gandhi, M. K., 147
George, Susan, 112n, 193
Germaine, Adrienne, 129, 183
Gerth, H. H., 93, 183
Gettens, John, 156n, 184
Gibbs, Christopher, 27, 184
Gilbert, Elon H., 113n, 184
Goldsmith, Arthur A., 83, 108, 184

Goldsmith, William, 87n, 196
Golembiewski, Robert T., 111n, 184
Gotsch, Carl H., 46, 184
Goulet, Denis, 82, 184
Gran, Guy, 93, 185
Grant, James P., 82, 185
Gray, Cheryl Williamson, 38, 185
Greeley, Martin, 129, 185
Gregersen, H. M., 85, 86, 185
Griffin, Keith, 112n, 185
Guha, Ramachandra, xii, 85, 185
Hageboeck, Molly, 101, 185
Hanke, Steve H., 101, 185
Haragopal, G., 84, 185
Hardin, Garrett, 100, 102, 186
Harrington, Larry, 178
Harrison, James Q., 110, 176
Hartfiel, Ann, 130, 186
Hatch, Charles, xii
Hatch, J.K., 190
Healy, Kevin, xii, 152, 156n, 169
Heermans, John G., 86, 186
Helleine, G. K., 120, 186
Hinton, William, 65n, 186
Hirschman, Albert O., 125, 186
Holwill, Richard H., 186
Hook, Richard M., 44, 195
Hoskins, Marilyn W., 52, 86, 129, 186
Hussain, Sajjad, 175
Hyden, Goren, 101, 186
Hyman, Eric L., 44, 111n, 124, 186
Ickis, John C., 111n, 187
Islam, A. K. M. Serajul, 175
Jain, Shobita, 85, 131, 187
Java, Ramesh, 8, 12n, 45, 102, 187
Jiggins, Janice, 33, 94, 179

Johl, S. S., 19, 187
Johnson, Ronald N., 101, 187
Johnstone, Bruce F., 39, 187
Juma, Calestous, 190
Karamchandani, Kanayo P., 12n, 160, 187
Kennedy, James, 29, 187
Khan, Akhter Hameed, 138-139
Khan, Asmeen, 12n, 187
Khan, Dilawar Ali, 107, 190
Kilby, Peter, 39, 122, 187, 188
Klauss, Rudi, 111n, 188
Kneerim, Jill, 83, 130, 188
Knight, Peter T., 37, 188
Kornher, Kenneth, xii
Korten, David C., xii, 23, 63, 78, 93, 95, 111n, 156n, 188
Krishna Murthi, B. V., 179
Kronick, J., 18, 188
Kurien, Verghese, 147, 149
Laarman, Jan G., 102, 188
Lamb, Geoff, 105, 193
LaPalombara, Joseph, 35n, 188
Liedholm, Carl, 122, 180
Lijencrantz, Christine, 129, 177
Lipton, Michael, 40, 189
Maddock, Nicholas, 101, 189
Mahar, Dennis, 188
Mahiti Team, 8, 12n, 189
Marcotte, Paul, 108, 189
Maru, Rushikesh, 187
May, Peter, xii, 77, 87n
Mayer, Albert, 23, 95, 142-143, 189
Mazumdar, Vina, 156n, 189
McKean, Margaret M., 102, 181
Mehen, Thomas, xii
Mellor, John W., 39, 189
Merkel, Albert, xii

Mickelwait, D. R., 190
Mills, C. Wright, 93, 183
Mnzava, E. M., 18, 189
Montagne, Pierre, 34, 95, 189
Moore, Mick, 110, 190
Morris, Morris D., 49, 190
Morss, Elliot R., 83, 190
Mudahar, Mohinder S., 19, 187
Murdoch, William W., 112n, 190
Myrdal, Gunnar, 43, 105, 125, 190
Narain, Sunita, 8, 12n, 163, 175
Nehru, Jawaharlal, 23, 142, 147
Nicholson, Norman K., 107, 111n, 190, 192
Norgaard, Richard B., 35n, 190
Norman, David W., 184
Nyerere, Julius K., 23, 150, 151
Oakerson, Ronald J., 195
O'Keefe, Phil, 35, 130, 190
Okonjo, Ramene, 130, 190
Olpadwala, Porus D., xi, xii, 135n, 164, 190
Ostrom Elinor, 102, 103, 111n, 191
Ostrom, Vincent, 111n, 191
Owens, Edgar F., 53n, 191
Pastore, J., 37, 191
Patel, Kalidas, 8, 160-61
Patel, Sardar Vallabhai, 147
Patel, Surendra J., 119, 191
Paul, Samuel, 156n, 191
Prosterman, Roy L., 62, 191
Quiros, Rodolfo, 161, 181
Raintree, John B., 62, 192
Ramaswamy, S. R., 179
Raphaeli, Nimrod, 35n, 192
Raulet, Harry M., 19, 192
Reddy, Arvind, xii

Reidigger, Jeffrey M., 62, 191
Resch, Tim, 30, 183
Reynolds, Norman, 44, 192
Riddell, James, 62, 183
Riker, James, xii
Riley, Bernard, 34
Robock, Stefan H., 126, 192
Roe, Emery, 83, 183
Rocheleau, Dianne, 131, 183
Romm, Jeff, xii, 6, 192
Rondinelli, Dennis A., 93, 94, 95, 108, 112n, 179, 192
Rostow, W. W., 49, 192
Roth, Gabriel, 101, 192
Russell, Clifford S., 111n, 192
Russell, John F. A., 179
Saint, William S., 160, 193
Savas, E. S., 111n, 193
Savonis, Michael, xii
Schaffer, Bernard B., 105, 193
Scott, James C., 81, 165, 193
Seers, Dudley, 83, 193
Shah, Tushaar, 102, 112n, 133, 193
Sharatchandra, H. C., 193
Shaw, Robert, 53n, 191
Shepherd, Gill, 12n
Shiva, Vandana, 42, 85, 102, 163, 193
Singh, Charan, 144
Sinha, Radha, 53n, 122, 193
Skutsch, M. M., 12n, 194
Slade, Roger, 110, 182
Smith, Brian C., 105, 112n, 194
Somjee, A. H., 156n, 194
Somjee, Geeta, 156n, 194
Spitz, Pierre, 41, 194
Stavis, Benedict, 19, 194
Stevens, Robert D., 192, 194
Stewart, Frances, 119, 120, 194
Streeten, Paul P., 49, 194
Sundar, Pushpa, 44, 192
Swanson, Louis E., 108, 189
Sweet, C. F., 190
Tai, Hung-chao, 53n
Thomas, Elizabeth Marshall, 55, 195
Thomas, John Woodward, 44, 195
Thompson, E. P., 123, 195
Thomson, James T., 63, 102, 111n, 195
Turnbull, Colin M., 55, 195
Uphoff, Norman T., xi, 49, 63, 74, 81, 82, 84, 87n, 93, 95, 111, 180, 181, 182, 188, 195, 196
Vaitsos, C., 119, 196
Visaria, Pravin, 9, 196
Wade, Robert, 28, 102, 165, 179, 196
Wallen, Suzanne, xii
Walsh, M. W., 38, 196
Wasserstrom, Robert, 83, 130, 196
Watt, James, 101
Weber, Max, 93
Wells, Louis T., 120, 197
West, Patrick C., 27, 30, 63, 94, 178
White, Louise G., 35n, 93, 108, 111n, 178, 197
Wiff, Mercedes, 131, 197
Williams, Robert G., 161, 197
Winch, Fred E., 184
Winkelman. Donald L., 178
Wood, Geoffrey D., 136n, 197
Zaror, Claudio, 42, 123, 176

INDEX OF SUBJECTS

Adaptive development administration, 92-97, 170
American Institute of Indian Studies, xi
Amul dairy scheme, 134, 137, 145-150
Appalachian region (United States), 124-125
Aswan dam (Egypt), 28
Ayni Ruway project (Bolivia), 137, 152-155
Bangladesh, 34, 95, 101, 124, 129, 132, 136n
Bangladesh Academy for Rural Development, 138
Bangladesh Rural Advancement Committee, 132
Berkeley, University of California at, xii, 34
Bihar state (India), 107, 145
Bolivia, 95, 130, 152-155
Brazil, 16, 37, 102-103, 118, 124, 126, 135n
Break points in the economic cycle, 116-118
Bucknell University, xi
Central America, 161
Centralization, 24-27
Centro Internacional de Mejormiento de Maíz y Trigo, 45, 108
China, 15, 51, 65, 90, 124, 135n
Chipko movement, 85, 107, 131
Collective action, 97, 102-103, 170

Comilla project (Bangladesh), 24, 137-141
Community Development program (India), 23, 24, 43, 95-96, 137, 141-145
Community forestry, defined, 11
Cornell University, xi, xii, 74
Corruption, 29, 165
Costa Rica, 95
Cultural Revolution (China), 51
Davis, University of California at, 32, 33
Decentralization, 4, 24-27, 103-107, 170
Development forestry, defined, 11
Dominican Republic, 131
Efficiency, defined, 53n
Egypt, 28, 40, 53n
Employment creation, 115-124
Employment Guarantee Scheme (India), 44, 52n
Equity and efficiency, 48-52
Eucalyptus, 10, 42, 162-163, 164, 167n
Farm forestry, defined, 11
Farming systems research, 4, 107-111
Food and Agricultural Organization of the United Nations, xi, 4, 8, 12n, 147, 167n
Food riots, 40
Ford Foundation, 139, 142
France, 90
Gal Oya irrigation project (Sri Lanka), 95, 111
Gambia, 130
Gezira scheme (Sudan), 28

"Green Revolution", 3, 45-47, 50, 52n, 107
Gujarat social forestry project, 6-11, 44
Gujarat state (India), 6, 12n, 145
Harijans, 146
Heritage Foundation, 101
Honduras, 131
Hong Kong, 118
Idaho, University of, xii
India, 15, 17, 30, 32, 35, 37, 85, 102, 124, 130, 131, 132, 162
Indian Scientific Institute, xii
Indigenous rural knowledge, 32-35
Indochina, 28
Indonesia, 16
Institution, defined, 69
Integrated rural development, 108
International Institute of Tropical Agriculture, 32
International Rice Research Institute, 21-22, 32, 45, 108
Ireland, 124
Italy, 124, 126
Jamaica, 80
Japan, 53n, 135n
Karnataka state (India), 161
Kenya, 34, 42, 95, 124, 130
Land reform, 62, 135n
Leucaena leucocephala, 18, 134
Linkages, 31-32, 58-60
Local organizations, 69-87, 170
Maharashtra state (India), xii, 44, 52n, 134
Malawi, 86, 95
Malaysia, 81

Mali, 34
Mexico, 16, 38, 118, 126
National Association of Schools of Public Affairs and Administration, xii
Nepal, 30, 86, 95, 102-103, 107
New Zealand, 147
Niger, 27, 30, 34, 86, 94-95
Nigeria, 16, 32, 130
Operation Flood (India), 146
Overseas Development Institute, 12n
Oxford Forestry Institute, xii, 34
Oxford, University of, 32, 33
Pakistan, 46, 63, 106, 138, 139
Panchayati Raj program (India), 107, 137, 141-145, 149
Papua New Guinea, 107
Parastatal bodies, 70-72
Participation, 82-87, 169
Philippines, 22, 79, 96, 124
PICOP (Philippines), 96, 124
Pilot projects, 21-24
Poland, 40
"Political will", 58
Privatization, 4, 97, 101-103
Production forestry, defined, 11
Proshika (Bangladesh) 132, 136n
Public choice, 97-103
Punjab state (India), 19, 28
Punjab state (Pakistan), 19
Purdah, 129
Quechua, 152, 155
Reagan administration, 101

"Redistribution with growth", 4
Regional and area development, 124-128
Regulation vs. promotion, 30-31
Rural institutions, 69-73
Russia, 90
Sahel, 35, 47, 86, 102, 161
Senegal, 30
Social Science Research Council, xi
Social forestry, defined, 11
South Korea, 17, 19, 85, 118, 135n
Sri Lanka, 81, 95, 111, 123
Sudan, 28
Swansea, University College of, xii
Taiwan, 19, 135n
Tanzania, 23, 42, 124, 150-152
Tennessee Valley Authority (United States), 126
Training and Visit system, 90, 107, 109-111, 165
"Trickle down", 3, 43, 49
Ujamaa movement (Tanzania), 23, 137, 150-152

United Nations Children's Fund, 147
United Nations Development Programme, 17
United States Agency for International Development, xi, xii, 101, 104, 139
United States, 90, 101, 124
"Urban bias", 40-42
Uttar Pradesh state (India), 145
Village Forestry Associations (South Korea), 85-86
Village Level Worker, 142
Water management, 28-29, 81
West Bengal state (India), 112, 133
Women in rural development, 128-131, 149
World Bank, 7, 9, 12n, 44, 93, 97, 101, 110
World Resources Institute, 5
"World shelf" of technology, 119
Yale University, xi, xii